PORNOGRAPHY AND SEXUAL VIOLENCE
Evidence of the links

PORNOGRAPHY AND SEXUAL VIOLENCE
Evidence of the links

The complete transcript of PUBLIC HEARINGS on Ordinances to Add Pornography as Discrimination Against Women: Minneapolis City Council, Government Operations Committee, December 12 and 13, 1983

Everywoman

First Published by
Everywoman Ltd, 34 Islington Green, London N1 8DU
Introduction © Everywoman Ltd 1988

ISBN 1 870868 00 5
Typeset by Contemporary Graphics Ltd, London
Printed by Cox & Wyman Ltd, Reading

ACKNOWLEDGEMENTS

This book could not have appeared without the financial support of the Cadbury Trust, for which we are grateful. The transcript of these hearings was first brought to our attention, as a document of great importance which could not be published in the United States, by Andrea Dworkin and considerable effort has been put into this by her and by Prof. Catharine McKinnon, both of who acted as professional consultants for the hearings.

In Britain, support and practical help has been given by Catherine Itzen, Sadie Robarts of ACTT, Clare Short MP, Michael Moorcock, Corinne Sweet, Martha Street and many others who encouraged this venture. We hope that it will justify the efforts involved, both in Britain where we are publishing it, and in the United States where it deserves to be widely read because of its specific concern with the issue of pornography in that country.

CONTENTS

Session III: Tuesday, December 13, 1983, 5.00pm.

Speakers:

Committee Members:
Van. F. White, Chairman
Walter Dziedzic
Patrick Daughtery
Sally Howard
Charlee Hoyt
Gerry Bruins, Clerk

Reporter:
Kimberley K. Kraemer (Janet R. Shaddix & Associates,
Bloomington, Minnesota)

INTRODUCTION

Why EVERYWOMAN is publishing this evidence

This book represents the publication of the first and so far only public hearings on pornography, which have allowed people to come forward with their evidence on the links between pornography and acts of sexual violence and abuse. The evidence includes studies of men to observe how their attitudes and behaviour change after viewing pornography, and personal testimony of rape and sexual assault which was directly linked either to the use of pornography by the assailant, or the manufacture of pornography from the assault.

Publication of this material, in the form of a complete transcript of the hearings held in Minneapolis City Council on 12 and 13 December 1983, is an historic event because strenuous efforts have been made since then to persuade a publisher in the United States to make them publicly available. It has proved impossible to persuade any publisher, in the very country where pornography is itself protected as "freedom of speech," to risk any association with evidence about its harmful effects on society — and especially on women and children.

This is one of many indications that in the United States, freedom of speech is available only to the assailants and not to the victims. The power and wealth of the pornography industry, and its interconnections with "respectable" publishing, distribution and sales outlets, mean the power to censor those who do not participate, do not agree with what is being said, and seek to expose the harm they are doing.

A freedom of speech which is available only to one side of an argument — whether because of government policy, money, or influence over the channels of communication — amounts to a censorship of critical or other points of view, and the promotion of what amounts to propaganda.

It is ironic that so soon after the publication in the United States

1

of Peter Wright's *Spycatcher*, a book about important issues in Britain which could not be published here because of censorship by the courts, we should be doing a similar job in reverse: defeating the unofficial but equally powerful system of censorship in the US of anything critical of pornography, by bringing it out in Britain both for our own debate here and for re-export to the States.

Many of those giving evidence did so at great personal risk, and we understand that there has been harassment and threats against some of them since the hearings. The names of some have therefore been deleted, to avoid making the situation any worse than it already is.

Pornography: new definitions

Because oppostion to pornography in Britain has been based almost entirely on the notion of "decency" versus "obscenity", and therefore attempts to censor frank discussion and depiction of anything sexual or erotic, it is crucial to make clear from the beginning how pornography was described and defined by the drafters of legislation for Minneapolis, for which these hearings were held, and also by those of us in Britain who have found this a useful approach which offers a breakthrough in discussions about the issue here.

Pornography is defined as a category which is quite distinct from sexually explicit or erotic material generally — which the proposed legislation in Minneapolis would not have affected in any way. The definition prepared by lawyers and campaigners in the US is, in the words of lawyer Catharine MacKinnon, specifically related to the subordination of women.

> *"We define pornography as the graphic, sexually explicit subordination of women through pictures or words, that also includes women dehumanised as sexual objects, things or commodities, enjoying pain or humiliation or rape, being tied up, cut up, mutilated, bruised or physically hurt, in postures of sexual submission or servility or display, reduced to body parts, penetrated by objects or animals, or presented in scenarios of degradation, injury, torture, shown as filthy or inferior, bleeding, bruised, or hurt in a context that makes these conditions sexual.*
>
> *"Erotica, defined by distinction as not this, might be sexually explicit materials premised on equality.*
>
> *"We also propose that the use of men, children or transsexuals in the place of women is pornography."**

---

*"Pornography, Civil Rights and Speech," Francis Biddle Memorial Lecture, Harvard Law School, 5 April 1984. The full legal definition, as worded (with some

The hearings and their US context

The Bill on which these hearings were held was the first attempt to allow those who are represented by pornography as victims to challenge those who profit financially from such representations. It was a Bill to allow individuals' complaints to be taken up by the city's Civil Rights Commission and was described as a Civil Rights measure, in terms of the Fourteenth Amendment to the United States Constitution which guarantees equal rights for all citizens. It was opposed largely on the grounds of the First Amendment, which guarantees freedom of speech. Thus the context was very different to that in Britain, where we have no constitution — but obviously the arguments on both sides are generally those which apply in Britain.

We need to ask ourselves why the First Amendment is seen by so many of the men speaking here as overriding all other amendments to the Constitution, which in principle have equal status. An enormous amount of money has been spent — by the pornographers in particular — on imposing the First Amendment at every opportunity against their critics, and in the process widening the definition of "speech" so that while rape, for example, is obviously a crime, deriving profit from a video of that rape is not because it is protected as "speech". Even if the rape has been committed with the main motive being to film the crime and then sell the film, no action can at present be taken to stop those sales, even though in many cases they identify to large numbers of viewers the victim of the rape — who in theory has the legal right to conceal her identity in order to avoid further assaults in imitation of the first.

---

minor variations) in a variety of ordinances, is:

"the graphic sexually explicit subordination of women through pictures and/or words that also includes one or more of the following:
(i) women are presented dehumanized as sexual objects, things, or commodities; or (ii) women are presented as sexual objects who enjoy pain or humiliation; or (iii) women are presented as sexual objects who experience sexual pleasure in being raped; or (iv) women are presented as sexual objects tied up or cut up or mutilated or bruised or physically hurt; or (v) women are presented in postures of sexual submission, servility or display; or (vi) women's body parts — including but not limited to vaginas, breasts and buttocks — are exhibited, such that women are reduced to those parts; or (vii) women are presented as whores by nature; or (viii) women are presented being penetrated by objects or animals; or (ix) women are presented in scenarios of degradation, injury, torture, shown as filthy or inferior, bleeding, bruised or hurt in a context that makes these conditions sexual."
In addition, all the ordinances also define "the use of men, children and transsexuals in the place of women" as pornography.

The situation in the U.S. now, where links between pornography and sexual violence are concerned, is nothing short of chaotic with double standards firmly entrenched in the law on the basis of the First Amendment. It is not a situation that we currently face in Britain, although we too lack any redress for individuals who feel they have been personally damaged by the effects of pornography. We also, of course, lack the possibility of a "class action" whereby a group of people who feel they have been misrepresented can take action. The draconian libel laws in Britain (which, incidentally, function very effectively as a means of censorship for those with the money to use them) are at the moment useless for our purposes. Although pornography, almost by definition, is extremely defamatory of those it portrays, the laws of defamation are geared to individual "reputation" in business or public life, rather than in the sense of personal safety.

The Minneapolis Bill, then, represents a most interesting innovation as the first proposed law to allow a legal challenge to pornography as a civil rights issue. The Bill was proposed as an amendment to the Civil Rights Code of the City of Minneapolis, Minnesota (although in the hearings there are references to its "twin city" of St Paul on the other side of the river). Public hearings are standard for Bills introduced at both State and Federal level in the United States, hence the opportunity for people in the area concerned to come forward with their evidence and views on the issue.

The City Council passed the Bill, following these hearings, on 30 December 1983. It was vetoed by the Mayor. The Bill was passed again with a few revisions in July 1984 — and again vetoed.

A similar Bill was presented to Indianapolis City Council, which passed it on 23 April 1984, and in this case it was signed by the Mayor and became law. It was immediately challenged by publishing trade groups, with support from civil liberties organisations which had made the First Amendment paramount in their policy, in the State of Indiana Supreme Court which has the power to overrule legislation if it is seen as "unconstitutional". On 19 November it overruled the new law on First Amendment grounds.

The supporters of legal action were obviously devastated by these wrecking tactics, after all their efforts to present their case and to argue it on civil rights (14th Amendment) grounds. There has been no further opportunity for legislation but a new model law has been prepared. It is drafted on similar lines to the Minneapolis Bill but would enable complainants to seek redress by going directly to court in a civil action. A further provision is also now being proposed: that grounds for suing pornographers should also include "defamation", as in libel actions, particularly for any use in pornography of a woman's name and/or likeness without her consent.

4

Bills along similar lines are being proposed in Norway and West Germany by women's organisations and civil liberties activists, and their prospects look much better than those in the US. There is some discussion in Britain too about the best ways to legislate on this issue, taking into account the specific legal context here.

The Minneapolis evidence

It only remains, then, to comment on the evidence given at the hearings whose transcript is reproduced here.

First of all, it is necessary to distinguish between evidence and proof. There are two different kinds of proof which could be said to apply to the links between pornography and sexual violence. One is scientific, although in the social sciences one is talking about something less categorical than in the physical sciences. Nevertheless, there are degrees of proof in this field which are generally accepted, such as high levels of correlation which are taken as proof of the link between smoking and cancer, for example. Dr. Donnerstein points out in these hearings that the evidence for linking pornography with sexual violence is considerably stronger than that for cigarette smoking and cancer (and much clearer than that linking violence on TV with violence in real life). This is clearly a debate for specialists rather than the general public, and the degree of proof required here is obviously a contentious one.

It should be borne in mind, incidentally, that many people accept without question the "fact" that pornography decreases the incidence of sexual violence by providing a harmless "release" for sexual excitement. No evidence at all is presented at these hearings in support of this hypothesis: on the contrary, it is argued that it flies in the face of all the findings in social science research about how people learn. It is being repeated endlessly, and perhaps believed as a result of the repitition rather than any proof.

The second kind of proof is the legal one, where evidence is heard on both sides and the case of one or other is deemed by the judge and/or jury to be "proven". This is quite a different matter, relying very largely on the credibility of witnesses, especially when recounting something directly experienced or observed or interviews with the accused. Although there is reference in these hearings, especially by Dr. Donnerstein,** to social science theory

---

**Since these hearings Dr. Donnerstein seems to have changed sides and now works for the pornography publishers and producers, repudiating (at least by implication) his testimony here. This may call into question the integrity of his own work, although his summary of other people's is more important here and remains equally verifiable by reference to the original researchers. As far as is known, none of them has objected to his summary of their findings about the effects on ordinary men of viewing pornography.

and proofs, the major part of these hearings is taken up by personal testimony such as would be given in a court of law: by the victims of rape and sexual abuse, by witnesses, including those living in areas zoned for pornography, and by those working with sex offenders who can speak with authority on their confessions and explanations of their crimes and the influence of pornography on them — and also on the prospects for reforming them.

What is clearly lacking is any systematic compilation of records, whether by the police or by those working with sex offenders during or after trial, which could serve as evidence of the connections between individuals' use of pornography and the commission of crimes of sexual violence.

This is a gap which could be filled immediately in Britain, since evidence about this issue would be relatively easy to collect and is so badly needed. Or is there perhaps some reluctance to collect evidence which may demonstrate the opposite to the "catharsis" theory, to which many cling with such conviction in their defence of pornography? It may well be the case that, just as the evidence given in the Minneapolis hearings proved so difficult to make public in the face of hostility from the publishing interests, so any suggestion that we collect evidence which is readibly accessible to police forces, prosecutors and those involved in rehabilitation of offenders will probably be unwelcome to those with a vested interest in producing, distributing and selling pornography.

EVERYWOMAN

It is important to note, also, that there is a mass of other evidence available on this issue arising out of research in the US and Canada, almost all of it still unavailable in published form. Although this kind of research does not seem to be going on in Britain or other countries, we know of other forms of evidence here which have yet to be collated and made public.

PROCEEDINGS

Prof. Catharine MacKinnon: defining pornography

CHAIRMAN WHITE: Having a quorum, the Government Operations Committee will come to order. One of the things that I would like to ask is that when there is a person who is presenting whatever they have of material in terms of verbalization, that there be no other comments because we do have a court reporter here who is taking it and when one or two or three people are talking, she can't get it down. So do it one at a time and let there be no other comments. This is not a debate, this is a public hearing. We are going to hear and receive the comments both pro and con from the audience.

The persons that are now about to take over will make their representations, they will make their comments, their slide presentations, and after that we will go into public comments.

It is in three stages. Today we go at 1:30 until 4:00 o'clock and we will reconvene at 5:00 o'clock and continue on, God Willing, it will be over by at least 7:00 or 8.00 o'clock. Tomorrow we have a 5:00 o'clock public hearing, the same continued public hearing. I would ask that the persons who are going to make comments and make presentations use the microphone at the very end of that table so that the television cameras can zoom in on you and do their thing.

Okay. Now, starting out, those that wish to speak, the sign-up sheet is right at that table (indicating), does anyone wish to sign up to speak? How many people in the audience are going to speak? Okay, we will allow three to four minutes in your speaking, we will try to hold it down because there are quite a few people who are going to speak.

Number one on the agenda is Dr. Edward Donnerstein.

MR. HYATT: Excuse me, may I speak before we get into Professor Donnerstein?

CHAIRMAN WHITE: Go ahead, City Attorney.

MR. HYATT: I am Allen Hyatt, Assistant City Attorney for

Minneapolis and I am assigned to this committee. Prior to the starting of testimony, we are going to hear from Professors Catharine MacKinnon, I believe, and Andrea Dworkin, both who are under contract to the City Council to develop an ordinance relating the violation of women's rights in regard to pornography to civil rights. And they have been asked by our City Council to develop that ordinance, they have done so, proposed ordinances before this committee and we will now hear from Professor MacKinnon.

Before we do that I would like to give you background. She is a Professor of Law at the University of Minnesota. She has, with Ms. Dworkin, conducted a course this year on pornography, particularly its effects on women, particularly the violent aspects of pornography. Eminently well qualified to speak on this topic and that is why we have contracted with her to do so. Professor MacKinnon.

MS. MacKINNON: As the committee knows, Andrea Dworkin and I are here today to discuss with you the proposed ordinance which we have drafted together under contract with the City to define pornography as what it is, that is to say as a violation of the Civil Rights of Women. We are proposing for your consideration a statutory scheme that will situate pornography as a central practice in the inequality of the sexes. In specific, as a practice that is central to the subordination of women.

This statute's principle arises under the Fourteenth Amendment which guarantees equality and freedom from discrimination to all citizens, including on the basis of sex. The concept of the systematic relegation of a group of people to inferiority because of a condition of birth that that idea should be — that those practices should be illegal, that idea is not novel in the context of the Fourteenth Amendment.

The understanding and the evidence which we will present to you today to support defining pornography as a practice of discrimination on the basis of sex is a new idea. I will be submitting to you, as soon as I am finished with this statement, a copy of my book which is a book about sex discrimination which made the argument that defined sexual harassment as a form of discrimination on the basis of sex, on the basis of a similar view, that is the same view of sex discrimination that underlies this ordinance.

In this hearing we are going to show the harm of pornography to women. What it takes to make it, particularly how it is used on people, from the coercion into making it to the effects of men consuming it which they act out on women, to the trafficking that provides both the movtivation and the access, to the harm of forcing it on someone to attempt to get them to perform sexual acts that they have no desire to perform, to seasoning children and prostitutes and wives and girl friends so that they will be more compliant sexually, so that they will become debased and lacking in self respect and lacking in existence and ideas of their own, to more direct assaults, stimulated, made desirable, and made legitimate and made sexy by pornography.

We plan to show why and how and in what sexual violence has become fun and sexy and entertaining and feminine and liberating and a definition

8

of love.

In particular, we want to show how the concept of pornography conditions and determines the way in which men actually treat women. Also the way men actually treat men and children.

We will show the ways that this abuse goes on in public as well as in private environments, and we will show that this is central to the way in which women remain second-class citizens in those environments, despite all our efforts to change that status.

We will document this on a national scale and in particular, replicate and show how everything that can be shown on a national scale is occurring now in the City of Minneapolis.

We will then argue that pornography has everything to do with why public policy is against some of the deepest injuries and injustices against women — that is to say sexual violence including rape, sexual harassment, battery, and prostitution — systematically have consistently failed women and we will argue why it is this ordinance will protect them.

The purpose of this hearing is principally factual. We think that we have found a large part of the way that women have been kept silent for a very long time and that is that pornography silences women. This hearing, this opportunity for our speech is precious and rare and unprecedented. That we can speak to our real injuries in a public forum is the kind of opportunity without which before now the guarantees of the First Amendment have not been useful to us. And they have not worked for us.

What I am saying is if pornography silences women, if it has already accomplished that silence, the First Amendment which prohibits the way that the state can silence people is not useful to us. When I say that the purpose of this hearing is factual, what I mean is that we will provide a factual basis for a legally sufficient sex discrimination statute, both in terms of the Fourteenth Amendment requirements and also to survive defenses that might be raised against it under the First Amendment. It is designed in both of those ways.

The primary purpose of the hearing, as I am understanding it now then, is not to advance legal arguments about why the statute withstands attack under the First Amendment although we believe that it will and I will be happy to respond to any questions that you have about that. But the primary purpose is to provide a factual basis so that it can withstand the defenses that most probably will be raised by principally the pornographers under the First Amendment.

Now, if asked, I am happy to address all —

MR. DZIEDZIC: Mr. Chairman, as one of the five committee members here I will tell you why I think we are having a public hearing. That is to gether input from the public about the issue so this committee could gather the input and we could go to the Council with a rational and intelligent suggestion on the issue. That is why we are having a public hearing.

MS. MacKINNON: Absolutely, that is exactly our purpose. And that in particular I think it is crucial that the people who are here to speak can be able to speak. I am not going to advance a lot of legal arguments to the

9

hearing, the purpose is factual and the people should be able to speak.

CHAIRMAN WHITE: That is on the onset what I was saying. We are here to receive and listen. If there is any written documentation I would like that to be passed up to the committee clerk so it goes into the record. I have some here too that I will give you.

But secondly, I would like to say I recognize the fact that there's going to be consensus which will bring about applause, I would ask that you would cease on that because it will slow down the process. It takes away from presenters in terms of what they are trying to say and it prolongs the hearing. So I will ask you to please not applaud whether you agree or disagree with a certain presenter.

MS. MacKINNON: I will also submit to you a copy of my book and my vita in that I am here as an expert consultant. Andrea Dworkin will make brief comments and then we will begin the testimony.

CHAIRMAN WHITE: Yes. What I am going to do is that you will make your presentation and then what I would like, since I don't have the knowledge of the three presenters that will be coming before us, I would like you, Professor MacKinnon, to introduce them and then we will continue.

Andrea Dworkin: dimensions of the problem

MS. DWORKIN: I would just like to situate the amendment that we have drafted in the context of international law. And in particular, in the context of the United Nations Convention on the elimination of all forms of discrimination against women from which I would like to now read briefly. Article 2 states, "State parties condemn discrimination against women in all its forms, agree to pursue by all appropriate means and without delay a policy of eliminating discrimination against women and, to this end, undertake to embody the principle of the equality of men and women in their national constitutions or other appropriate legislation if not yet incorporated therein and to insure, through law and other appropriate means, the practical realization of this principle. To adopt appropriate legislative and other measures, including sanctions where appropriate, prohibiting all discrimination against women. And protect the legal rights of women on an equal basis with men." And it goes on in that vein which I think is clear.

Article 6 specifically states, "State parties shall take all appropriate measures, including legislation, to suppress all forms of traffic in women and exploitation of prostitution of women."

Now, I want to make clear the dimensions of the problem that we are talking about. Pornography is part of the traffic in women. In this country it is a seven billion dollar industry that buys and sells women's bodies. I am going to put into evidence two pieces of literature. One is a magazine article from the magazine *Aegis*, called "The Political Economy of Pornography" that describes the actual economic dimensions of the industry. And I quote from the article, "If all of this material were produced by a single corporation, 'Pornography Incorporated' at seven billion dollars a year would be the fortieth largest company on the Fortune 500, as large as Xerox, RCA, or Bethlehem Steel." In addition, I would like to suggest that pornography is an industry based entirely on the domination of women by men and that this description of the material now available is accurate from the same article, "At least 25 percent of all the heterosexual material sold in Washington's 'adult' bookstores, for example, depicts explicit violence against women — torture of all kinds, whipping, beating, mutilation, rape, and murder. Not all the violence is vicarious; the stores also stock everything from whips and chains to 12 inch spiked plastic penises, so that the customers can participate directly. The hard-core material has become increasingly sadomasochistic during the past few years, but even the basic soft-core presentation of unequal, one-sided nudity (vulnerable, exposed women with fully clothed or unseen men) conveys a very clear message of male sexual dominance. Such one-sided nudity is commonly used by men to dominate and humiliate other males in prisons and military training, and has the same psychological effect when applied overwhelmingly to women in culturewide media like soft-core pornography."

In other words, we are dealing with an endemic and systematic dominance of men over women, that is the subordination we are trying to address.

I would also like to submit into evidence a copy of my book which is a description of the actual content in the pornography that is being produced at this time.

I thank you very much for this time, and we will now advance with the testimony.

CHAIRMAN WHITE: I would like to state with these presentations you have an hour each. I read that to mean that within this time frame from 1:30 to 4:00 o'clock that this will be cut down, you will not speak for one hour each.

MS. MacKINNON: No, the understanding is that that is the amount of time given to each of those experts. They will speak in some cases only for say 15 minutes and then there will be questions from the Council, in some cases questions to us in attempt to clarify the relation between their testimony and this ordinance.

MR. DZIEDZIC: Chairman, just so there is no misunderstanding, we have 12.

MS. MacKINNON: That is this evening.

MR. DZIEDZIC: We have 10 other people that wish to speak.

MS. HOYT: That is tonight.

MR. DZIEDZIC: Sorry, that is tonight.

Dr. Ed Donnerstein: An outline of the research

MS. MacKINNON: Dr. Donnerstein, are you ready?

Dr. Donnerstein, if you could begin by identifying yourself and I will submit your vita.

DR. DONNERSTEIN: I wonder, can I be heard in the back of the

11

room without a mike? Can you hear me?

My name is Ed Donnerstein, D-o-n-n-e-r-s-t-e-i-n. I am a psychologist at the Center for Communication Research at the University of Wisconsin, Madison, 200 miles south and a bit warmer.

What I want to present into evidence is an outline of some of the major topics I wish to cover with some of the major references in scientific literature, also allowing some space for notes by the City Council. And four major book chapters, discussing overviews of the major research in the last 10 years on the effects, particularly the effects of sexual violence or aggressive pornography or pornography in general and the effects it has on attitudes towards women about rape and aggressive behaviour. There are essentially six topics, really five, I would like to cover and it is going to be a little difficult, I think, given the slide projector,* but I will try and I hope the gentlemen and the women on the City Council will see them. I apologize to members of the audience who can't.

The six topics are as follows, in terms of dealing with the relationship with sexual violence in the mass media on attitudes on rape and attitudes on aggression. Number one, what are the images and secondly, is there an increase in the media? The answer is going to be a definite yes and I will give some brief descriptions very shortly.

Secondly, what are the effects of this type of material on a number of things. One, what are the effects of sexual violent images or aggressive pornography on sexual arousal in rapists, known criminal offenders, and more importantly, quote unquote normals? I will describe what I mean by that shortly.

Thirdly, what are the effects of this type of material on rape related attitudes? The attitudes meaning myths about rape stereotypes, willingness for a person to say they would commit a rape and attitudes in general about women.

And fourthly, what are the effects of this type of material on aggressive behaviour, primarily aggressive behaviour against women in a laboratory type situation which is, of course, the only place one could conduct such a research.

Fifthly, what is the relative contribution of sexual and violent contents of the material. I think what the research tends to indicate, this is not an issue of quote unquote sexual explicitness or nudity. It is a question of how women are portrayed, particularly women as victims which we are really talking about.

Finally, what are the effects of massive long term exposure to this type of material?

Let me make a preface here. We are going to be talking about initially short term exposure in a research contact. Short term is five or ten minutes of exposure, primarily to very normal types of male subjects. I think you will see even with that some fairly dramatic type of results.

When we get to long term exposure I think you will see the effects are

---

*The slides are not reproduced here.

even stronger, particularly with the types of material which have no physical violent context. That is the straight type of pornographic or erotic material. So keep in mind a number of things. One, when I mention in this research that there are no effects in the short term for erotica, we are talking about material made by myself or other colleagues, material which is sexually explicit and does not show power orientation between males and females.

When we talk about aggressive pornography we are talking about material in which women are abused physically and in which there are acts of rape, mutilation, or other types of physical aggression. We will talk about the long term effects of this type of material.

Number one, what are the images? Let me give you examples of what we are talking about. We have what is classified as obviously nothing to do with pornography at all to the hard-core effects. We have three or four images which will suffice.

(Slide show being shown.)

DR. DONNERSTEIN: This, I think, has nothing to do with pornography but I think the message is very clear. We find it as a common scenario in most of the common material. This is a slide of a woman who is tied up, bound black and blue. It is nothing more than an advertisement for a Rolling Stones album cover. I think it is interesting, the woman is saying a scenario we find in a great deal of pornography. I am black and blue from the Rolling Stones and I love it. Violence is a sexual turn-on, that is the message which consistently comes through in this type of material. And what we are going to say is that without question that has very, very strong effects, particularly on adolescent males and males who are beginning to form certain types of stereotypes about human sexuality, about rape and violence.

The next slide I call subtle, it might be my own desenitization, I think it represents the over-the-counter magazine, *Hustler,* which depicts violent types of images against women. I think it deserves no other comment, but it is a subtle image compared to the types of graphic violation we will get to very soon.

This gets a little closer to the hard-core market. I should admit that every one of these slides I have, you can find in almost every city. In fact, the next slide you don't have to go to an adult bookstore to find. I am not sure you have to find this in an adult bookstore either. I think it gets a little more toward the violence.

The next slide I have a blank, I show it to only demonstrate the excessive types of sex against women. Until we started on a recent science foundation project, I found this is not excessive. I think a number of people will find it bit difficult to look at, I don't mean it to offend anyone, I don't mean it to show anger to anybody. I think you have to have some ideas about the type of material we are talking about when we talk about aggresive pornography. This type of material is readily available. I present it to show that the research will show inclusively that many healthy males become sexually aroused to this type of image.

Now, the question is what are the effects of this type of material? Like we just saw, the first question is what are the effects on sexual arousal and there are a number of reasons why, I would like to discuss that.

I have a quote up there from Neil Malamuth who is at UCLA and basically what he says, I can't read the quote, I am going to have to paraphrase it. Basically what Malamuth says that if individuals become sexually aroused, which is a very positive state, we are not saying there is anything wrong with sexual arousal, if they become aroused from scenes of rape in the media, in pornography that is: number one, do they become sexually aroused? Would they go ahead and make the attribution that if they engaged in such behaviour it would be a sexually arousing experience? Those are a number of conceptual leaps.

First of all, you have to determine whether or not quote unquote normal, healthy males could conceivably become sexually aroused to brutality, scenes of rape, scenes of mutilation.

Secondly, even if they did, would they go ahead and make the attribution that number one, I would like to engage in such behaviour and secondly, if I so did, it would not only be sexually arousing for the victim, which in fact it usually is shown that way, that it would be sexually arousing for myself?

Let's ask the first question, is the material sexually arousing and who is it sexually arousing to? Most of the early research dealt with the effects of this on a rapist. It was widely assumed that rapists would be sexually aroused by images of rape in the media. If you look at the graph up in the front, you see an example of a rapist and the nonrapist population. Rapists were shown films which depicted rape or films of mutually consenting intercourse. A group of nonrapists were shown similar types of materials. When and what the researchers did was look at sexual arousal, penile tumescence in males. Basically what they found is that rapists do in fact become very sexually aroused to violent images. Images of women being aggressed against in the sexual content. The assumption, however, was that normal males, not convicted of a sexual crime, do not show the same type of reactions. The assumption is that normals would not become sexually aroused to this type of material.

A few years ago Neil Malamuth at UCLA conducted a large amount of studies — by the way I am mentioning one percent of the research in this area to get through it — but Malamuth found if you take normal males and present them with a scene of rape from pornography but you present them with the common type of scenario which is a woman enjoying being raped, when a woman is violated, aggressed against, she becomes sexually aroused. What Malamuth found was, one, normal healthy males also became sexually aroused when they viewed that type of image. If you present them with a highly explicit erotic film they become sexually aroused. If you present them with a scene in which a woman is raped but doesn't become sexually aroused, the majority of males would not become sexually aroused. But most normal males, when you present them with a scene of rape and the only differences between the scene on the left and the other scene is right at the end of the rape, even though the violence is the same, the victim shows sexual arousal which again is a common type of scenario one finds in the material. You find normal males becoming sexually aroused to these type of image.

Let's go on for a second. Malamuth has found, as have we and other researchers, that there is a scale called the Rape Myth Acceptance Scale. It touches many of the common types of myths which individuals hold about rape. Any woman who hitchhikes deserves to get raped, women unconsciously set up situations which force rape on them, women enjoy being raped, women who wear provocative clothing are putting themselves in a place to get raped: these are common myths held by rapists. It is held as an instrument to determine if treatment for a rapist was satisfactory.

What you find is that after only 10 minutes of exposure to aggressive pornography, particularly material in which women are shown being aggressed against, you find male subjects are much more willing to accept these particular types of myths. In fact, this particular slide again shows a good example of that.

Male subjects or female subjects were shown a sexually violent film in which a woman is raped and gets turned on to the rape. After they had seen this film a week later, they are more accepting of these types of myths and more accepting on an Acceptance of Interpersonal Violence scale. That scale has items, as: it is justified to hit your wife or spouse, the only way to turn a woman on is through force, and that women find aggressiveness a sexual turn-on. You find, after exposure of this type of material, more acceptance of these types of myths.

Another interesting thing, if you look at Neil Malamuth's research, you also find some other changes in attitude. This particular study showed that if male subjects were presented with a rape depiction that is aggressive pornography, that is if a woman shows a positive reaction, I apologize for having to use that term, it is a term that is used meaning that the victim in the scene becomes sexually aroused, you find again that normal, healthy male subjects say the following. If asked, "What percentage of women do you know who enjoy being raped?" — think about the question for a second, think about the context of how this research is done. You find normal males, after five minutes of exposure to pornography, say 25 percent of the women they know would enjoy being raped.

Secondly, what percentage of women do you know who enjoy being aggressively forced into sexual intercourse? Again we are not talking about rapists, not talking about sexual deviants; talking about normal, healthy male college students at Manitoba, UCLA, Bloomington and other places. Thirty percent of the women they know would enjoy being aggressively forced into sexual intercourse.

The most important question of all is questions that ask subjects, after esposure to this material, what is the likelihood that you would commit a rape if I guarantee that you won't be caught? Think about that for a second, you are asking a normal, healthy male would you commit a rape after exposure to this type of material — and on a five point scale you find that after exposure to sexually violent images, particularly when those sexual violent images depict women enjoying rape, up to 57 percent of

15

those males indicate some likelihood they would commit a rape if not caught.

In fact, in the general population as it turns out, anywhere between 25 and 30 percent of normal, healthy males indicate some willingness they would commit a rape. And in fact if you look at those individuals, and I think it is important to do so very quickly, you find a number of interesting things about them. Again, this is the normal distribution of at least male college students.

One, they believe other men would rape if not caught. They identify with the rapist, basically meaning if you put them in a situation which involves a rape there is good likelihood they would never convict the rapist. They believe that, one, rape victims cause their own assaults; two, derive pleasure from their assaults. It is associated with rape, with aggression against women.

More important than that, if you take the 25 or 30 percent, we are not talking about a small minority but a large percentage of people. Particularly when you think about the amount of people that might see any particular film, even if it is only one percent, we are talking about an incredible amount of potential harm to women. Twenty-five to thirty percent, if you take these individuals and if you look at the bottom graph that measures sexual arousal, the likelihood to rape people, meaning those are males, that 25 percent indicate that they would commit a rape. Basically you find those particular males, again normal males in the population, not rapists convicted or sentenced in any way, those particular males are sexually aroused to all types of rape images. They are sexually aroused to rape images which give the images that is women enjoy being raped. More importantly, that they are sexually aroused to the graphic forms of violence against women. Even if it doesn't show these quote unquote positive reactions.

In fact, if you take a good close look at that bottom graph, you find that those 25 to 30 percent of the male population are much more sexually aroused to that scene of rape than they are to erotic types of material. Futhermore, if you ask these males would they find committing a rape sexually arousing, the answer is yes.

Now, what does this say about sexual arousal and attitudes? It says, number one, there is a substantial amount of normal, healthy males who can become sexually aroused to violent images, particularly in which the woman is shown to experience pleasure. Again the common scenario. More important than that, there was at least 25 percent of the male population who would commit a rape if not caught. We are not saying they would in fact commit a rape, except there is high correlation between items which I have just talked about and the use of actual physical force admitted by these individuals. And in fact, if you use the same scales on known offenders you would find the same data.

I am not going to make that leap that this would predict actual rape. It predicts attitudes about rapes by offenders. That 25-30 percent are aroused to all forms of sexual violence against women, not only finding it arousing but are willing to admit they will commit that type of act because it would be arousing for them.

Secondly, what type of an effect does this type of material have on aggressive behavior against women? There is a lot of research that shows if you expose male subjects to specifically violent erotica you find increases in violent behavior. Let me give a quick example. This is a study in which male subjects saw neutral type of films, erotic films that we constructed or a standard type of aggressive film in which a woman is raped. In one condition, she shows a great deal of pleasure from getting raped. In another we had to construct ourselves, there was a negative ending. The interesting thing is, the scene was identical. You are showing normal males a violent type of scene and if you look at the bottom data, how many women did suffer when male subjects saw the women enjoying the rape, she enjoyed it less. She enjoyed it more when there was more done. It the woman was raped but there was a positive reaction at the end, she is seen as being more responsible for what happened. There is no difference between the positive and the negative ending of those films, the violence against the woman, the pain and suffering, the brutality is identical. The only thing is, one takes on the common pornographic scenario that violence is a turn-on to the victim. What do males do, normal males? They see less violence. In fact, after exposure to that type of material — by the way if you take the same males, sit them in a room an hour later and ask them to think of something sexually arousing and write it down as soon as they become sexually aroused and write down what they are thinking about, what do you think their passages are? They are scenes of rape. That is what is becoming sexually arousing for them: violence. There is nothing wrong with sexual arousal, the problem is its juxtaposition with violence.

What happens after a few conditioning trials is, as soon as you begin to remove the sexual content and leave the brutality and the violence, what do you find? Sexual arousal. In fact, in Abel's research at New York University you can predict how violent a rapist is in terms of did they in fact mutilate and murder the victim, in terms of how sexually aroused they are, not to scenes of sex but to scenes of simply violence against women.

In our research we are not talking about rapists, we are talking about normal, healthy, young males. What happens in terms of aggressive behavior? You find, for instance, that the erotic films have no effect. Again when I talk about erotica, I am talking about films we put together ourselves. They show sexual explicitness, no power, anything of that nature. When male subjects are angered and exposed to a scene of rape, whether it has a positive or negative ending, as you can see from the dotted line on the top, they are aggressive against the female. If you show them a violent scene in which there is a positive ending, in which they have not been angered, they are less aggressive against females.

Let me point out, I have been in the area of aggression for years. Those of us who have worked in media violence or television will say one thing: it is almost impossible to find individuals becoming aggressive when they see violent films unless they have been angered or predisposed. Here we have a group of subjects who are not angered of predisposed. Yet after seeing several types of sexually violent material, particularly the common scenario in which women enjoyed being brutalized, enjoyed being raped, you get increases in aggressive behavior. Keep in mind throughout all of this, I think it will be more clear shortly, we are not dealing with hostile people, we are not dealing with a prison population of sex offenders. We are dealing with normal healthy males.

By the way, I don't mean to complicate things, my professional remarks always come out in some of this.

That is a little more complicated graph than it should be but I present it mainly because of a number of things. Somebody asked me, I think in a news conference, about objectivity. The best way to show objectivity is by replication of other people. A lot of the research I have been talking about has been done by mainly other people. I will talk about my research shortly.

This shows if you can measure sexual arousal to sexual images and meaure people's attitudes about rape, you can predict aggressive behavior with women, weeks and even months later, that is what it shows. And what we know is that this type of material does lead to sexual arousal and it does lead to changes in attitudes. Once you have found those you can predict aggressive behavior.

We are not talking about correlations where we get into chicken/egg problems of which came first, we are talking about causality. The ability at least at this research to take certain types of images, expose people to those images and make a prediction independent of their background, independent of their past viewing habits, independent of their initial hostility and make quite accurate predictions of potential aggressive behavior. We have obviously come a long way, at least as researchers. I think it suggests quite strongly there are strong relationships between the material and subsequent aggression.

In fact, good colleagues of mine would argue that the relationship between particularly sexually violent images in the media and subsequent aggression and changes in or toward callous attitudes towards women, is much stronger statistically than the relationship between smoking and cancer — mainly because most of that research is correlational. This is not.

Another quesion: what are we really talking about? Are we talking about the effects of sexual explicitness or the effects of violence against women? We are talking about the effects of violence against women, at least in the research we have been doing. Let me briefly mention one study in which we went ahead and took normal males. They saw a sexually explicit film, a film which depicted violence against women or a film which only presented violence against women. Besides looking at aggressive behavior we asked the subject's feelings about rape and if they would have used force to have sexual acts against women or if they would have raped a woman if not caught. At the bottom there is erotic material, you find that both the aggressive-erotic and aggressive films increased attitudes about rape in a negative direction and in fact, 50 percent of our subjects said they would not commit a rape if not caught, if they saw just the aggressive film. It is not so much the sexual content, it is however the role of the women in the film. However, many subjects when they see a woman aggressed against will see sexual content.

If you look at the aggressive behavior you find the same thing. The erotic film in and of itself, that is a film that ends with intercourse between sexually consenting adults, it does not lead to violence. The aggressive film does, whether or not the people are angered or not angered, and so does the aggressive-erotic film.

Let me end up talking, in the last couple of minutes, about the long term research. Researchers like myself and Neil Malamuth at UCLA are looking at massive long-term exposure to this material. some interesting things occur. If you expose male subjects to six weeks' worth of standard hard-core pornography which does not contain overtly physical violence in it, you find changes in attitudes towards women. They become more callous towards women. You find a trivialization towards rape which means after six weeks of exposure, male subjects are less likely to convict for a rape, less likely to give a harsh sentence to a rapist if in fact convicted.

In our own research we are looking at the same thing. Let me point out one thing. We use in our research very normal people. I keep stressing that because it is very, very important. What we are doing is exposing hundreds and hundreds of males and now females to a six-week diet of sexually violent films, R-rated or X-rated or explicit X-rated films. We preselect these people on a number of tests to make sure they are not hostile, anxious or psychotic.

Let me point out the National Institute of Mental Health and the National Science Foundation and our own subjects committee will not allow us to take hostile males and expose them to this type of material, because of the risk to the community. They obviously know something some of us do not.

What we do is take these males, and we prescreen them. That represents — and I again apologize for getting so technical, I want to point out how normal those males are, That is a straight line on top which represents our population. The line underneath represents the males we chose. As you see, they are below the mean. More than that, this is a scale that runs from one to four; a score of one means you possess some of these traits, as you can see our chosen people possess none of these traits. They are so normal, incredibly normal, that there is no risk. This works against us in what we are doing.

These males are then shown a number of films. Let me give you the names, okay, they are porn. They are R-rated films, *I Spit On Your Grave, Maniac, Toolbox Murders, Vice Squad, Texas Chainsaw Massacre,* and others.

The X violent are commercially released films. They have scenes of overtly physical violence. They are: *Captain Lust, Defiance of Good, Sex Wish, Easy, Dirty Western.*

The X-rated films, the violence in them, if there is, is not seen by the subjects. Such films are: *Health Spa, Debbie Does Dallas, Other Side of*

Julie. They see them over a two-week period.

Let me, by the way, if I can read the one quote, I think it is important. This comes from a video cassette. Here is the advertisement for one of our R-rated films. "See blood thirsty butchers, killer thrillers, crazed cannibals, zonked zombies, mutilating maniacs, hemoglobin horrors, plasmatic perverts, and sadistic slayers slash, strangle, mangle, and mutilate bare-breasted beauties in bondage!" Unfortunately there is truth in advertising, that is what you get. I think one should keep in mind this material is for a young audience, this is for 15, 16-year olds rather than those that are 18. We study 18 year olds.

Some examples: this material is classic. Women are killed in sexual ways, in the bathtub or shower as in *Psycho*-gone-astray films, things have gotten explicit. Every time a woman is killed it has a sexual overtone. It is to get the audience sexually aroused, and juxtaposition with sexual forms of violence. Of course, the classic *Texas Chain Saw* — let me give you an example from one of these. This comes from *Tool Box Murders:* basically in this scene we have an erotic bathtub scene. A woman in the bathtub massaging herself. There is a beautiful song, *Pretty Lady,* it is a nice country-western song that comes on. In two minutes the psychotic killer comes in. The woman notices him, he is carrying a long, what is called a nail gun, it drives nails through walls, a power nail gun. The music stops. He chases her around the room and in fact again it exemplifies the typical type of scenario. When men are killed they are killed swiftly, no sexual overtones. Whem women are killed it is dragged out indefinitely. He shoots her through the stomach with the nail gun. She falls across a chair. He then comes up to her and the song *Pretty Lady* comes back on as it did when she was taking the shower, or excuse me, in the bathtub. He puts the nail gun to her forehead and blows her brains out.

Again, I think we have got to think about the audience watching this film, it is a young audience. There is nothing wrong with the bathtub scene, there is nothing wrong with sexual explicitness. What is wrong is it's incredible, it is in juxtaposition with some of the graphic violence available. And yes, young males will become sexually aroused with the images. If you remove the sexual context, unfortunately they will become aroused to the violence.

After subjects and since — by the way, I have colleagues here who are lawyers. After they had watched two weeks of the films, they are brought to our law school and they see a documentary of rape, *State of Wisconsin versus David Tyler.* It is a re-enactment of a real rape trial. They sit in the trial as jurors. We were not interested in the rape behaviour, we were interested in the men's thoughts on violence with women and how they view women. I think what you will see is desensitization. This is our victim. During the testimony into the trial a physician who attended to the victim presents into evidence a picture of the victim after she was raped and this is passed out, by the way, to these male jurors. Again, two weeks after exposure to this type of material, what do we find?

Basically what they show is the same thing. Let me go through quickly. Here are the subjects' moods on a daily basis, you see over a time less depressed, less annoyed or bothered by forms of graphic violence. If you ask them about particular perceptions of violence, if you look at the same films from day one to day five, if it is one week or two weeks, they see less blood and less blood and gore and less violent scenes. Over time they find the material more humorous, they are less depressed, they enjoy the material more and are less upset. You also find the same things for the X violent films, those are X-rated in which the main scene is women being raped, women being bound, hung, aggressed against in general. You find that subjects find less violence, as time goes on, against women in these films over repeated exposure. They are just as sexually aroused over this, however, to the material. Sexual arousal does not decrease. They feel much less likely to censor the material, they are less offended by the material, they see this less graphic and less gory, they look away less. What that means, on the first day when they saw women being raped and aggressed against, it bothers them. By day five it does not bother them at all, in fact they enjoy it.

If we look again how upset: they were less upset and less debased and they found the material makes a great deal of sense and was more meaningful by the end of the week. I am not sure what is exactly meaningful. If we look at how offensive the material is, it is much more offensive on day one than day five. The violent material was very degrading on day one, much less degrading on day five. If we look, as time went on they found it less and less degrading until the fifth day; there is a reason for that. We happen to tell them we will show them a double feature and we don't do that. They find the material less degrading with time.

We have a film called *Vice Squad*. If subjects saw that film on day one, on day one they see a lot of scenes of rape, on day four nothing has changed in the film. They see half the amount of rape, they become desensitized to what rape and violence is. This represents their recollections to the one and a half hour rape trial. We are a long way from completely analyzing this data.

On the last day we bring in a control group of subjects who have never seen the films. We ask how injured the woman was. Subjects who have seen violent material or X-rated material see less injury to a rape victim than people who haven't seen these films. Furthermore, they consider the woman to be more worthless than any of them who have not seen this material. There are a number of other correlations which I am going to summarize because of time.

Basically, what happens is the less violence the subjects see, the less sexually aroused they are and less bothered by the material after one or two weeks of exposure. The more they say the woman is responsible for her rape, the more less likely to convict the rapist. The less injury they see on the part of the victim, the more worthless they see the individual.

Let me make a 30-second closing statement. What does all the research say? Well, compared I think to 1968 when we had the Pornography Commission, I think it says many different things.

One, the material has changed quite drastically. Secondly, the research techniques we have as researchers have also changed. I think we are asking many different questions today than years ago. Unfortunately, I think it shows that short-term exposure to very normal, sociable, intellectual young males is going to have an effect. It is either going to reinforce already existing predispositions about rape in women and maintain these callous types of attitudes or worse than that, in fact, change them in a very negative direction and that is the majority of the subjects. Unfortunately there is out there a small percentage — and I hate to use the word minority — who are so influenced by this material that it becomes the ultimate sexual turn-on. Individuals are becoming sexually aroused to the trivialization, the degradation, and the use of women. The data, I think it speaks for itself. I am not a lawyer, I am not an advocate, I am unfortunately a "ivy tower" professor that does his research. I think the data is a little too clear, not only from myself but dozens of professors across the country, I doubt that anybody disputes the data. There are effects. Thank you.

CHAIRMAN WHITE: I feel that I would like to ask you a question. In terms of your research, is the typicals of your research beginning to reach out not only to women showing this love affair with violence, is it not pointing also to men and children? I just ask you that question. In other words, is it affecting men?

DR. DONNERSTEIN: In fact, our research works only at the effects it has on women. A number of my graduate students who are women are now conducting research, independent of myself, on the effects which this material has on women and the effects are more dramatic. Our issue is how it affects men, not only in terms of how it affects their aggressive behaviour. We can't expose the material to them and see if they go out and commit a rape. We are much more interested in effect how it affects our attitudes, attitudes about women, attitudes with human sexuality, our attitudes about violence in general. And the issue of desensitization of violence is not new. There are thousands and thousands of studies. We can't show them violence, it would purge all this aggressive energy. There is no research in the academic community which supports that, there never has been and there never will be. It is a theoretical issue. I am not just talking about my research, by the way, we are talking about thousands upon thousands of studies. Theoretically if it is men leading to desensitization against men or violence against children or violence against women, the same thing is going to occur.

More important than that, I think we have got to realize it, if you assume that your child can learn from Sesame Street how to count one, two, three, four, five, believe me they can learn how to pick up a gun and also learn attitudes. I think the concern should be, what attitudes are they learning about male/female relations? Unfortunately, their attitudes are influenced with too much degradation and violence.

MS. MacKINNON: I have a couple of questions.

Dr. Donnerstein, could you explain why it is that your research comes to conclusions that are so different than the conclusions of the

Commission on Obscenity and Pornography in 1970?

DR. DONNERSTEIN: Ms. MacKinnon, it is not my research, it is everybody's. But the material has changed. The Pornography Commission made a concerted effort not to deal with violence images. In fact, there were a couple of studies that eroticism leads to aggression. That they made a concerted effort to get away from violence. They are asking questions we don't ask today. They were looking at short term effects. You are not going to find people's attitudes changing overnight. It is going to take a long time.

What the research is doing today, thanks to the national support from Mental Health and the Science Foundation, is to allow researchers to look at pornography which is drastically different and allow us to look at it with long-term type of exposure. I think for the most part that is why the results are different.

Let me comment, Professor MacKinnon, many of the people who were on the commission that did the research, they have also changed their mind.

MS. MacKINNON: Could you also describe just very briefly what you are seeing: how do you characterize the long-term effects of the X only?

DR. DONNERSTEIN: One of the problems I think, in our own naiveté is, we thought nonviolent X-rated material would lead to aggression with five minutes of exposure. The material presents more subtle types of images which are going to work at stereotypes, and certain myths about women. What we find as soon as you get into long-term exposure to this material, you begin to get these types of changes. You may not necessarily get definite relations to aggressive behaviour because that is going to be a little longer to do, I think eventually we are going to get there.

You get increases in sexual stereotypes and pretty much exactly the same things in terms of the attitudes that you get with the violent material. The only difference is the immediate increase in aggression. That is really where the differences occur.

MS. MacKINNON: And is your research the first research to complete this study of long-term effects of this kind of material?

DR. DONNERSTEIN: Will, I think both ours —

MS. MacKINNON: Particularly X?

DR. DONNERSTEIN: Zillmann has, but that was reported a few years ago. Basically the research by Zillmann stated that exposure did produce arousal. Unfortunately, when you show them a scene of rape they became sexually aroused. There was some selective exposure.

Basically, when they looked at attitudes, it was the attitudes that were changing over the long run in a very subtle way. We can't expect, as we did with the violent material which is so graphic, to get an immediate effect. What we are finding is the longer exposure you begin to get subtle changes in attitudes toward women.

Let me bring this up. Zillmann happens to use the Sex Callousness Scale. The Commission found with one hour of exposure there were no changes in sexually calloused attitudes, the same as violence. Those sexually calloused attitudes are correlated with violence if you read the scale. With six weeks of exposure, when you have the funds to do the research, you in fact find an increase on the part of males of sexually calloused type of attitudes.

CHAIRMAN WHITE: I want to thank you for your presentation, you articulated it well. You have a vast reservoir of research to share with this committee and with the audience.

MS.MacKINNON: Andrea Dworkin has one question.

MS. DWORKIN: I would like Dr. Donnerstein to address the fact that there has been a lot of general studies of violence in the media and I would like to know if it is proper to say, from what you have told us here, that the study of the impact of pornography is very specific and concrete in ways that are distinguishable from the general environment?

DR. DONNERSTEIN: In fact the effects are much stronger and occur much more rapidly. I think the interesting thing is, if you take a look at the research and really talk about hundreds and hundreds of studies — I present them into evidence, a number of chapters which have all these bibliographies — there is an incredible amount of consensus across populations and measures and studies.

That I think is interesting, because in the media violence area we have some ambiguity and the relationships are statistically not as strong as they are here. So yes, I agree with you.

MS. DWORKIN: Thank you.

MS. MacKINNON: Thank you, Dr. Donnerstein.

CHAIRMAN WHITE: Thank you very· much, I hope you can stick around and listen to others.

Linda Marciano: the myth about "Linda Lovelace"

MS. MacKINNON: Next is Linda Marciano.

CHAIRMAN WHITE: All right. Now prior to Ms. Marciano's speaking, I would ask there be no discussions during this because once again, to reiterate, the stenographer is taking down testimony.

You now have the floor, if you wish to begin.

MS. MacKINNON: We are trying to arrange so that you can see the witness.

Go ahead.

CHAIRMAN WHITE: Give your name and spelling for the stenographer.

MS. MARCIANO: I feel I should introduce myself and tell you why I feel I am qualified to speak out against pornography. My name today is Linda Marciano. Linda Lovelace was the name I bore during a two and a half year period of imprisonment. For those of you who don't know the name, Linda Lovelace was the victim of this so-called victimless crime.

Used and abused by Mr. Traynor, her captor, she was forced through physical, mental and sexual abuse, and often at gunpoint and threats to her life, to be involved in pornography. Linda Lovelace was not a willing participant but became the sex freak of the '70s.

24

It all began in 1971. I was recuperating from a near-fatal car accident at my parents' home in Florida. A girlfriend of mine came to visit me with a person by the name of Mr. Charles Traynor. He came off as a considerate gentleman, asking us what we would like to do and how we would like to spend the afternoon and opening doors and lighting cigarettes and all so-called manners of society.

Needless to say I was impressed, and started to date him. I was not getting along with my own parents. I was 21 and resented being told to be home at 11:00 o'clock and to call and say where I was, and to call and give the phone number and address where I would be.

Here comes the biggest mistake of my life. Seeing how upset I was with my home life, Mr. Traynor offered me his assistance. He said I could come and live at his home in Miami. The relationship was platonic, which was fine with me. My plan was to recuperate and then go back to New York and live. I thought then he was being kind and a nice friend. Today I know why the relationship was platonic. He was incapable of a sexual act without inflicting some type of pain or degradation upon a human being.

When I decided to head back north and informed Mr. Traynor of my intention, that was when I met the real Mr. Traynor and my two and a half years of imprisonment began. He began a complete turnaround and beat me up physically and began the mental abuse; from that day forward my hell began.

I literally became a prisoner. I was not allowed out of his sight, not even to use the bathrom. Why, you may ask. Because there was a window in the bathroom. When speaking to either of my friends or my parents, he was on the extension with a .45 automatic 8-shot pointed at me. I was beaten physically and suffered mental abuse each and every day thereafter.

In my book *Ordeal*, an autobiography, I go into greater detail of the monstrosity I was put through. From prostitution to porno films to celebrity satisfier. The things that he used, to get me involved in pornography, went from a .45 automatic 8-shot and M-16 semi-automatic machine gun to threats on the lives of my family. I have seen the kind of people involved in pornography and how they will use anyone to get what they want.

So many people ask me: Why didn't you escape? Well I did, I'm here today. I did try during the two and a half years to escape on three separate occasions. The first and second time I was caught and suffered a brutal beating and an awful sexual abuse as punishment. The third time I was at my parents' home and Mr. Traynor threatened to kill my parents. I said, "No you won't, my father is here in the other room" and he said, 'I will kill him and each and every member of your family." just then my nephew came in through the kitchen door to the living room, he pulled out the .45 and said he would shoot him if I didn't leave immediately. I did.

Some of you might say I was foolish, but I'm not the kind of person who could live the rest of my life knowing that another human being had died because of me.

The name, Linda Lovelace, gave me a great deal of courage and notoriety. Had Linda Borman been shot dead in a hotel room, no questions would be asked. If Linda Lovelace was shot dead in Los Angeles, questions would have been asked. After three unsuccessful attempts at escaping, I realized I had to take my time and plan it well. It took six months of preparation to convince Mr. Traynor to allow me out of his sight for 15 minutes. I had to tell him he was right, a woman's body was to be used to make money, that porno was great, that beating people was the right thing to do. Fortunately for me, after I acquired my 15 minutes out of his presence I also had someone that wanted to help me.

I tried to tell my story several times. Once to a reporter, Vernon Scott, who works for the UPI. He said he couldn't print it. Again on the Regis Philbin Show and when I started to explain what happened to me, that I was beaten and forced into it, he laughed. Also at a grand jury hearing in California, after they had watched a porno film they asked me why I did it. I said, "Because a gun was being pointed at me" and they just said "Oh, but no charges were ever filed."

I also called the Beverly Hills Police Department on my final escape and I told them that Mr. Traynor was walking around looking for me with an M-16. When they first told me that they couldn't become involved in domestic affairs, I accepted that and asked them and told them that he was illegally possessing these weapons, and they simply told me to call back when he was in the room.

During the filming of *Deep Throat,* actually after the first day, I suffered a brutal beating in my room for smiling on the set. It was a hotel room and the whole crew was in one room, there was at least 20 people partying, music going, laughing and having a good time. Mr Traynor started to bounce me off the walls. I figured, out of 20 people there might be one human being that would do something to help me and I was screaming for help, I was being beaten, I was being kicked around and again bounced off of walls. And all of a sudden the room next door became very quiet. Nobody, not one person came to help me.

The greatest complaint the next day is the fact that there was bruises on my body. So many people say that in *Deep Throat* I have a smile on my face and I look as though I am really enjoying myself. No one ever asked me how those bruises got on my body.

Mr. Traynor stopped searching for me because he acquired Marilyn Chambers, who I believe is also being held against her will.

A reporter from the Philadelphia newspaper did an interview, his name is Larry Fields. During the course of the interview Ms. Chambers asked for permission to go to the bathroom and he refused it. Mr. Fields objected and said, why don't you let the poor girl go to the bathroom, she is about to go on stage and he came back with "I don't tell you how to write your newspaper, don't tell me how to treat my broads."

I have also been in touch with a girl who was with Mr. Traynor two months prior to getting me, who was put through a similar situation but not as strong. And as it stands today she still fears for her life and the life of her family. Personally, I think it is time that the legal system in this country realize that one, you can't be held prisoner for two and a half

26

years and the next day trust the society which has caused your pain and resume the life you once called yours. It takes time to overcome the total dehumanization which you have been through.

It is time for something to be done about the civil rights of the victims and not criminals, the victims being women. But realize, please, it is not just the women who are victims but also children, men and our society.

CHAIRMAN WHITE: Thank you for your testimony, Ms. Marciano. I would like to say, because of time again, there are those who are a little irate that they are here thinking that they would have the opportunity to participate in this public hearing by getting in a comment. So I think we are going to have to be expeditious in terms of questions and answers, we should move this right along so we give people who are here this morning, who will not have the opportunity this evening, to have their day to speak. So would you begin?

MS. DWORKIN: Thank you, I will try to do that.

Ms Marciano, I have to ask you some questions that are difficult for me to ask and I apologize to you for asking them. It is important that we get the answers.

Could you describe for us the first time that Mr. Traynor prostituted you?

Ms. MARCIANO: It happened in Florida. I had thought we were going to visit a friend of his and we pulled up to a Holiday Inn. So my second reaction was a buffet, I thought we were going to lunch. And he took me up to a room and there was five men in the room and told me that I was there to satisfy each and every one of them. And I said that I wouldn't do it so what he did is he took me into this little dressing area and he told me that if I didn't do it that he would shoot me. And I said, you won't shoot me, there is five men in this room, you just won't do it, somebody will say something and do something. And he just laughed hysterically. He said that my body would be found and I would be another prostitute who was shot in her hotel room or something like that and that none of the men would do anything, they would just laugh.

During this event I started to cry and while these five men were doing whatever they wanted to do, and it was really a pitiful scene because here I was, they knew I wasn't into it. One of the men complained and asked for his money back because I was crying and I wasn't the super freak that Mr. Traynor usually brought around. And he was given back his money. And the other four men proceeded to do what they wanted to do through my tears and all.

MS DWORKIN: Thank you, Ms. Marciano. One of the major themes in pornography is that women are portrayed having intercourse of — doing various —

MR. DAUGHTERY: Could you speak into the mike, ma'am?

MS. DWORKIN: One of the situations that is commonly portrayed in pornography is women being — women having sexual intercourse and doing various sex acts with animals. You were forced to make such a film, could you describe for us the situation in which you were forced to make this film?

27

MR. DAUGHTERY: Would you like to respond?

MS. MARCIANO: Yes, I think it is important that everyone understands.

Prior to that film being made, about a week, Mr Traynor suggfested the thought that I do films with a D-O-G and I told him that I wouldn't do it. I suffered a brutal beating, he claims he suffered embarrassment because I wouldn't do it.

We then went to another porno studio, one of the sleaziest ones I have ever seen, and then this guy walked in with his animal and I again started crying. I started crying. I said I am not going to do this and they were all very persistent, the two men involved in making the pornographic film and Mr. Traynor himself. And I started to leave and go outside of the room whey they make these films, and when I turned around there was all of a sudden a gun displayed on the desk and having seen the coarseness and the callousness of the people involved in pornography, I knew that I would have been shot and killed.

Needless to say, the film was shot and still is one of the hardest ones for me to deal with today.

MS. DWORKIN: Thank you, I am sorry but this is something that I had to ask.

There was one other incident that you described in your book *Ordeal* that involved Mr. Hefner, Hugh Hefner at the Playboy Mansion, that was about the same theme. Would you tell us briefly about that?

MS. MARCIANO: Yes. Well, we first met Mr. Hefner. Mr. Traynor and him sat around discussing what they could do with me, all kinds of different atrocities. And it seemed that Mr. Hefner and Mr. Traynor both enjoyed seeing a woman being used by an animal. And so Mr. Hefner had Mr. Traynor's dog flown in from Florida to the L. A. Mansion. And one evening they decided that it was time and they had one of the security guards bring the animal down to Mr. Hefner's bathhouse and fortunately, during my two and a half years in imprisonment there was a girl that tried to help me in her own sort of way. She told me the tricks to avoid that kind of situation and I did what I could to avoid it but Mr. Traynor and Mr. Hefner were both very disappointed.

MS. DWORKIN: Thank you. Would you explain to us how it was that Mr. Traynor taught you to do what is now known popularly in this culture, because of the movie *Deep Throat,* as the sex act of deep throating?

MS. MARCIANO: Well, he used hypnotism. He told me that it would overcome the natural reflexes in your throat that would prevent you from gagging and it was through hypnotism that I was able, I guess, to accomplish the feat, I guess you could say.

MS. DWORKIN: So that hypnotism was added to the prostitution?

MS. MARCIANO: Yes, it was.

MS. DWORKIN: My final question is this: Some people may think that you could have gotten away, for instance, when Mr. Traynor was sleeping. Could you explain to us why that was impossible?

MS. MARCIANO: Well, at night what he would do is put his body over my body so that if I did try to get up he would wake up. And he was a very light sleeper. If I did attempt to move or roll over in my sleep he would awaken.

MS. DWORKIN: Thank you very much.

MS. MacKINNON: How do you feel about the existence of the film *Deep Throat* and its continually being shown?

MS. MARCIANO: I feel very hurt and very disappointed in my society and my country for allowing the fact that I was raped, I was beaten, I was put through two and a half years of what I was put through. And it's taken me almost 10 years to overcome the damage that he caused.

And the fact that this film is still being shown and that my three children will one day walk down the street and see their mother being abused, it makes me angry, makes me sad. Virtually every time someone watches the film they are watching me being raped.

MR. DAUGHTERY: All right. Catharine, do you have another witness?

MS. MacKINNON: We were going to allow the space for a member of the public who was given the wrong information. She is not part of what we were going to proceed with. We thought it was best to be more brief with Ms. Marciano so that this woman could speak.

We have a couple of documents to submit.

MS. DWORKIN: May we do that first?

MR. DAUGHTERY: Thank you, Mrs. Marciano, for showing up.

MS. MARCIANO: Thank you. I would like to say thank you for everybody who made it possible for me to be here tonight. I want to speak out for what happened to me and for the other members of society. I feel that it is important that victims have a chance today in our society. And I also want to say that my children thank you.

MS. DWORKIN: I would like to just put into evidence in support of Linda's testimony, we will be providing you with a copy of her book *Ordeal* which tells the facts. We are also providing you with a copy of her lie detector test that bears out the truth of everything that she has said to you today.

In addition, I would like to read a letter by Dr. Kathleen Barry who is a Professor of Sociology and who is an author of the book *Female Sexual Slavery*. We will also put this into evidence:

"In this memo I intend to identify the practices related to pornography which constitute a violation of women's civil rights, and in accordance with the International Declaration of Human Rights, they constitute a violation of women's human rights. As I have already conducted, reported and published the research in this book," she goes on to say that she is not going to reiterate all of the conclusions.

"Number one, pornography is used by pimps as part of the illegal acting of procuring and attempting to induce young girls and women into prostitution by presenting young women and girls with pornography which fraudulently represents actually painful sexual practices and acts as pleasing and gratifying to the female represented in the pornography. The pimp attempts to convince young and vulnerable, usually homeless, young women to prostitute themselves for him. Pornography plays a large role in the deception that is necessary to put naive young women into prostitution.

"When a young girl or woman is procured, pornography is often used as part of the seasoning and blackmail strategies which will force her into prostitution. Prior to being 'turned out' to prostitution, many pimps 'season' or break down their victims through sessions of rape and other forms of sexual abuse. Sometimes these sessions are photographed or filmed and used in a variety of ways which include personal pleasure of the pimp and his friends, blackmailing the victim by threatening to send them to her family, and selling them to the pornographers for mass production. This constitutes the use of pornography as a form of torture and the marketing of actual torture sessions in the form of film and pictures as a pleasure commodity.

"Pornography is a form of prostitution and consequently pornographers are pimps. There have been several court cases upholding the convictions of pornographers as pimps for having been supported off the earnings of prostitutes."

That is a small portion of Kathleen Barry's letter, which I will submit with her book.

I would also like to read just two paragraphs to you from the U.N. report on the suppression of the traffic in persons and the exploitation of the prostitution of others. I will also put this into evidence.

CHAIRMAN WHITE: Ms. Dworkin, I would like to — I hate to continually talk all the time, if you could just submit them for the record. The media, if they wish them, they can get them from the committee clerk and so we can move right along.

MS. DWORKIN: Thank you.

There is one other point I want to make. I won't read the whole letter, I will tell you we have a letter here from a New York crisis worker about the increased existence of rape of the throat, since the distribution of the movie *Deep Throat*. And in addition the increased use of cameras in actual rape situations.

CHAIRMAN WHITE: We are going to move quite quickly now.

Ms. Marchiano, I want to thank you for coming to testify.

MS. MARCIANO: Thank you very much.

Dr. Pauline Bart: what men learn from pornography

CHAIRMAN WHITE: We have Dr. Pauline Bart who will utilize as little of the time that has been allotted to her, if she can make it precise as possible I would appreciate that. We do have speakers and it is rather long, we will give people an opportunity to speak for three minutes. We have a young lady out here with a baby, I would like her to go first after Mrs. Bart.

Dr. Bart is a Professor of Sociology, Abraham Lincoln Medical Center, University of Chicago (Chicago Circle). Would you tell me what Chicago Circle is before you begin?

DR. BART: Well, I agree, it is rather complex.

I have spent the last 20 years studying gender, studying what happens to women and what happens to men and women and children because of the problem of gender inequality in this country, beginning with depressed middle-aged women, Portnoy's Mothers, what gynaecologists say about women in their textbooks, and abortion.

For the past 10 years I have been studying rape and rape avoidance. This was a study funded by the National Institute of Mental Health. In the course of focusing on rape and the injury it causes I, as other researchers in sexual assault such as Dr. Russell and Dr. Scully, realized that we had to learn about pornography for reasons I will discuss below.

I must say that it is a pleasure to be in the Minneapolis/St. Paul area which has in so many ways led the way in having data-based public policy on preventing child sexual assault, on battery, the study on arresting the batterers, having the first women's shelters in this country. I hope fervently that will follow with pornography. My pleasure is increased by the knowledge that my city celebrated Hugh Hefner Day last week.

My presentation will deal with the following themes: Pornography as harm to women, including its use to socialize men in gender and inequality; very briefly critiques which purport to show that pornography is harmless and the study of audience response to a film about pornography, data which clearly indicates that women believe pornography injures us as a class.

When I first came to the University of Illinois Medical School and I sat in on a sex education class I learned that they were, and I saw that they were, being shown pornography to desensitize what they might hear about in their practice. I know there are some of you that are insensitive enough as it is and, of course, most of us are aware that as part of medical school education, the physicians' futures, physicians were shown pornographic slides intermixed with the ordinary anatomy slides to liven up the lecture. Professor Myra Marx Ferree at the University of Connecticut told me, and I then called her on December 6th to get words that I could use for you, that when they went around to the various dorms to tell them the relationship between pornography and violence against women, particularly rape, Professor Donnerstein has participated in collecting and has presented an argument made to rebut her argument, but one of the male students made an argument that pornography was not harmful. In fact they were interested in getting the porno films on campus at the beginning of the fall semester because the freshmen guys did not know how to relate to women and you have to show them. And they said that, you know, Professor Ferree was talking about the relationship between pornography to bad things. You're talking about relationships to normal men, not to rape. It is really about normal sex. So I think that the use of this as a teaching device should be something we should investigate.

A recent study by Strauss and Behr, University of New Hampshire, they did a relationship between the sales of sex magazines and the rate of rapes reported to police from the crime reports and they found that "Pornography induces attitudes that increases the likelihood of rape."

The correlation in '79 was .63 and the correlation in 1980 was .58. For those of you who are familiar with the social science literature, these are substantially high correlations.

The work Zillmann, who had been mentioned before, showed that explicit sexual behaviour films shown to students over an extended period showed that at the end they, the ones who saw the films, were more hostile to the women's movement, that is to the equality of women, and suggested lower sentences for rapists than those who saw neutral films or saw half neutral films and half sexually explicit films.

Diana Russell, who I mentioned before, in her random sample of women in San Francisco, found that 10 per cent said yes when she asked them "Have you ever been upset by anyone trying to get you to do what they have seen in pornographic pictures, movies, or books?" Now, maybe they were wrong and the guys didn't get the idea from pornography. On the other hand, similarly maybe they were asked to do things that they did not know that came from pornography, so the 10 percent figure is one we can become comfortable with.

Let me tell you some of the things that they have been asked to do because of pornographic pictures — and this was by their husbands and boy friends. (And on the basis of some prior research I did, I can tell you that research done by people we trust, excuse me, that sexual assault done by people whom you trust is worse than sexual assault done by a stranger. Your trust, your judgment, everying about you is violated more than if you have the kind of rape that everybody would agree is a rape.)

"Miss A: Urinating in someone's mouth."

"Miss B: It was a three-girls-and-him situation. We had sex. I was really young — like 14."

"Miss C: He was a lover. He'd go to porno movies, then he'd come home and say, 'I saw this in a movie. Let's try it.' I felt really exploited, like I was being put in a mold."

"Miss D: I was staying at this guy's house. He tried to make me have oral sex with him. He said he'd seen far-out stuff in movies, and that it would be fun to mentally and physically torture a woman."

"Miss E: It was physical slapping and hitting. It wasn't a turn-on; it was more a feeling of being used as an object. What was most upsetting was that he thought it would be a turn-on"

"Miss F: He'd read something in a pornographic book, and then he wanted to live it out. It was too violent for me to do something like that. It was basically getting dressed up and spanking. Him spanking me. I refused to do it."

"Miss G: He forced me to have oral sex with him when I had no desire to do it."

"Miss H: This couple who had just read a porno book wanted to try the groupie number with four people. They tried to persuade my boy friend to persuade me. They were running around naked, and I felt really uncomfortable."

"Miss I: It was S and M Stuff. I was asked if I would participate in being beaten up. It was a proposition, it never happened. I didn't like the idea of it."

"Interviewer: Did anything else upset you?"

"Miss I: Anal intercourse. I have been asked to do that, but I don't enjoy it at all. I have had to do it, very occasionally."

"Miss J: My husband enjoys pornographic movies. He tries to get me to do things he finds exciting in movies. They include twosomes and threesomes. I always refuse. Also, I was always upset with his ideas about putting objects in my vagina, until I learned this is not as deviant as I used to think. He used to force me or put whatever he enjoyed into me."

"Miss K: He forced me to go down on him. He said he'd been going to porno movies. He'd seen this and wanted me to do it. He also wanted to pour champagne on my vagina. I got beat up because I didn't want to do it. He pulled my hair and slapped me around. After that I went ahead and did it, but there was no feeling in it."

"Miss L: I was newly divorced when this date talked about S and M and I said, 'You've got to be nuts. Learning to experience pleasure through pain. But it's your pleasure and my pain'. I was very upset: The whole idea that someone thought I would want to sacrifice myself and have pain and bruises. It's a sick mentality. This was when I first realized there were many men out there who believe this."

"Miss M: Anal sex. First he attempted gentle persuasion, I guess. He was somebody I'd been dating a while and we'd gone to bed a few times. Once he tried to persuade to go along with anal sex, first verbally, then by touching me. When I said 'No' he did it anyway — much to my pain. It hurt like hell."

"Miss N: This guy had seen a movie where a woman was being made love to by dogs. He suggested that some of his friends had a dog and we should have a party and set the dog loose on the women. He wanted me to put a muzzle on the dog and put some sort of stuff on my vagina so that the dog would lick there."

"Miss O: My old man and I went to a show that had lots of tying up and anal intercourse. We came home and proceeded to make love. He went out and got two belts. He tied my feet together with one, and with the other he kind of beat me. I was in the spirit, I went along with it. But when he tried to penetrate me anally I couldn't take it, it was too painful. I managed to convey to him verbally to quit it. He did stop, but not soon enough to suit me. Then one time he branded me. I still have a scar on my butt. He put a little wax initial thing on a hot plate and then stuck it on my ass when I was unaware."

"Miss P: My boy friend and I saw a movie in which there was masochism. After that he wanted to gag me and tie me up. He was stoned, I was not. I was really shocked at his behaviour. I was nervous and uptight. He literally tried to force me, after gagging me first. He snuck up behind me with a scarf. He was hurting me with it and I started getting upset. Then I realized it wasn't a joke. He grabbed me and shook me by my shoulders and brought out some ropes, and told me to relax, and I would enjoy it. Then he started putting me down about my feelings about sex, and my inhibitedness. I started crying and struggling with him, got

33

loose and kicked him in the testicles, which forced him down on the couch. I ran out of the house. Next day he called and apologized, but that was the end of him."

As may be clear from some of the quotations cited, there was often insufficient probing by the interviewers to determine the exact nature of the unwanted sexual experience. That is, the number of clear-cut cases reported is likely to be a considerable understatement and we can't of course prove by this that the pornography caused this kind of behaviour, but it is like the relationship, in this case the correlation, between smoking and cancer. I would suggest that these women, as well as the women in my study that I will talk to you about, may well study what is called Post Traumatic Stress Syndrome in the diagnostic and statistical manner which we are veterans in the cases of, which we are very familiar with. They have nightmares, loss of appetite, the kind of things that women who are injurated have experienced, and it goes on for a long time. Let me talk a little bit about the women in my study and then I will talk about attitudes in response to Linda Lovelace's story.

I spoke to 43 women who had been raped. Many of the men denied that what they were doing was raping. One man said, "I am not raping you, you are raping me." And another said, "You entered this place of your own free will." And one man said, "There is no such thing as rape." Now sociologists, you know, use big words to explain things and the word we use is neutralization. It is used to justify the kind of behavior originally that was enjoyed by juvenile delinquents and it involves denial of responsibility and denial of injury.

Now denial of injury was the most common rationale the men used. Let me tell you what the women told us that the rapist said: "You are going to enjoy this" as he raped her at knifepoint.

"I know you won't mind what I do to you," as he was displaying a gun.

"I don't want to rape you, I just want to screw," as he locked her in his room penetrating her anus and vagina with his fingers.

"You know there is no such thing as rape, a man is doing a woman a favor." This is a man who had conned a woman into his apartment and forced her to have oral sex and masturbate him.

"You are going to feel good, I am going to penetrate you," said a cab driver viciously trying to rape his passenger.

Said he "wanted to make love" but if she did not co-operate he would kill her. This was said by a naked man holding a knife, mounted on a sleeping woman. He left saying, "Here I was trying to be nice." He also said that he was shy and it was too bad that they had to meet this way.

And the last quote is: "You will feel better when I am inside you."

Now, men aren't born believing this, they have to learn it some place and I maintain that one of the ways they learn it is through pornography. The women told me that frequently they were asked or demanded to state how much they were enjoying the rapes, and that was harder for them to do than the act, than experiencing the actual rape.

One of my friends was raped with a gun to her head, and her rapist insisted that she have an orgasm. He then wanted her to have another

34

orgasm and then backed down, he said well, she might be a little tired from the first one. As if rape itself isn't enough of an injury, these women were further injured by the lie which academics call ideology: that women enjoy forced sex and enjoy forced pain, and this is the ideology that is presented in pornography. That is one of the reasons that I got into studying pornography.

The third part of the study that I am going to report, third study, has to do with audience research on *Not a Love Story*. Before I do so, I want to simply briefly recapitulate what Professor Donnerstein said about the Commission Report.

There were two records that came out the same time, one on violence and one on pornography. The one on violence was based on ordinary learning theory, which is a substantial theoretical perspective inside psychology, and the theory is: the more you see the more you do.

The one on pornography, however, came out with a different explanation, the catharsis model, which was: the more you see the less you do. And as we have been so eloquently spoken to, there is absolutely no data for the last analysis.

I have written a paper which I think has been submitted to you called "Dirty Books, Dirty Films, and Dirty Data" that addresses the issue. And all I can say is that if any of my students ever did any research as shocking as that research which has been so quickly picked up and put into textbooks and is still there, you ask people what they think and do, where they learn that pornography was harmless, I would feel that I had failed as a teacher. If indeed it were true that the catharsis model is successful, then since we have had a proliferation of pornography we should have a diminution of sexual assault and rape and that is certainly not the case.

I did the only study, to my knowledge, that has been done on a more or less national audience. This is, I didn't use students in my class and I didn't call a group together. I studied people who went to see *Not a Love Story*, a film about pornography. The ads just said "a film about pornography". Word got out that it was an anti-pornography film but not everyone who came to see the film came thinking that. I did not have a random sample and I certainly would not claim that I had a random sample. However, that in a sense strengthens my findings because the sample was biased in exactly the way that would be associated with people who would be pro-pornography. They were young and they were well educated compared with the general population. And we know from prior research that this group generally has a more permissive attitude towards pornography.

I read this in the *New York Times* yesterday: they apparently removed from the park a bronze entitled "Playmates" showing three boys gazing at a centerfold of a *Playboy* magazine. In the centerfold was a black view — excuse me, a back view, also a black view of a woman wearing a scanty négligée. There was opposition on some part of the communities and kids were seen giggling about it. And the sculptor said, "Actually the piece was not designed to have kids elbow each other and giggle. It was to have adults reminisce a bit about this stage of their development." I suggest

35

that it did not allow the women to reminisce a bit about our development.

Okay. What I want to basically tell you, and the rest of the stuff is submitted, will be submitted, is that what I have found in setting out *Not a Love Story* it's the siting for a big study of sex of the audience over a month period.

My findings were that men and women have very different attitudes towards pornography. Men didn't like it very much and women hated it. There was particular differences on two issues. One was that pornography has — the question was: "Do you think pornography has its place?" Women and men really split with most women saying no, it didn't. They strongly disagree. Seventy-two percent disagreed strongly.

One the question of rape, "Some of the increase in the rate of rape can be attributed to pornography," 81 percent of the women agreed and 51 percent of the men agreed.

The scientific study of sex has changed. When I showed the film *Not a Love Story* and had a panel with Donnerstein, Malamuth, Stock and Abel, even in this group I found there was similar differences between males and females. There were 40 percent of the men strongly agreeing that there was a place for pornography but only 11.5 percent of the females agreeing.

I will just close with a poem, because I think it is the poets that get at the essence of our experience, not the academics. It is a poem called "Homage to Virginia Woolf", who as you recall walked into the rivers and drowned.

"I am thinking of a woman who walked into the waters of a river with stones in her pockets. I am thinking of the waters of the river of my life. I am thinking of the stones in my pockets, all women are born with stones in our pockets, empty them, empty them, empty them, swim.

MR. DAUGHTERY: Pauline, one second.

MS MacKINNON: I think for the sake of time, Chairman, in order to preserve as much time as possible to the public I won't ask for any other questions.

I will submit one document, which is a letter from a doctor who recently went to a medical school and found pornography still being used in the training of gynaecologists in sex education. To document that it is still going on. Thank you.

CHAIRMAN WHITE: I want to thank you. I was out of the room but I will tell you and the audience that there are speakers in all the other rooms. We are not slighting anyone when we are running back and forth.

Jane Strauss: Concerns of a book-seller

It is now public hearing time and there is a lady here with her child who wishes to speak. And what is her name? Jane Strauss.

I would like to say three to four minutes in your presentations so that we can move right along. We are getting close to the time that we are supposed to be breaking, we may have to go over a little bit.

If you will begin by giving your name and address to the stenographer and to the committee clerk.

MS. STRAUSS: First of all, thank you very much, Mr. White for making this possible. We were a little confused about times here and the baby is getting a little restless.

I am Jane Strauss, S-t-r-a-u-s-s, I live at 3120 Third Avenue South. I am coming here with two concerns and I will try to be as brief as possible.

The first concern is I am a parent trying to raise a child in South Minneapolis. Just recently, well, at the present time the place where we live is within five blocks of two pornography stores and two health clubs, 24-hour girls in lingerie. I have some concerns from that standpoint. I have some concerns that my husband and I own some legitimate bookstores in which a small, very small percentage of what we carry, which is asked for by some of our customers, is things which might be considered to be pornography under this ordinance. And I have some concerns with regard to that, with regard to small business people who are trying to survive as compared to the Alexanders who make their living exclusively from the pornography, degradation of men, women, and children.

I have read over the proposed ordinance several times. I have shown it to my spouse who, say what you will, he appears to be a man but who is an attorney by training and to several other attorneys whom I know, some of whom are women. One of my concerns is that this deals only with pornography per se. One of the major concerns that I see is the presence of prostitution and yes, pornography may encourage that. There is no direct provision with regard to the presence of prostitution in this. I am concerned about that, I am concerned about probable discriminatory stuff. The definition which is given in the ordinance points to degrading pictures of women, it is women in this and women in that. We have here men, seen in *Buns,* available in B. Dalton or lots of other places. We have gay-oriented pornography. I find this offensive; it is not covered. We have *Playgirl,* that is men. My God, I don't think it is that great, it is stuff that is commonly available. It is stuff that you can get at the local magazine wholesaler, at the local book wholesaler in this town.

I also have some concerns that violence is no less violent because it is violence against men. That focusing on a male crotch as an essence of that person is not less demeaning than focusing on a female crotch or breasts. I have some concerns about that.

The second thing — another thing I have a concern about is that no distinction is made between a full-line bookstore or convenience store that has *Playboy* and *Penthouse,* maybe, and an operation like that owned by the Alexander Brothers which their primary purpose is peddling pornography. I think there is a distinction in kind of those two. You may disagree, but this is my concern.

Another concern that I have is that, for example, if three out of 20,000 titles are offensive to somebody in a full line bookstore, the person who owns that bookstore is still liable to suit. From a purely practical viewpoint it is not physically possible to read absolutely everything that you stock in that store. I will show you, these are romance novels; the

37

current trend in category romance novels is for increasingly graphic things. Many who are thinking women would find those quite offensive, I do. On the other hand, there are women who buy and devour three or four a week and this is the market at which these are aimed, young women, 16 to 40 or 16 to 35, many of whom are housewives and things like that. I don't just think it is real appropriate.

I am concerned that this could possibly open the way for a large number of suits at personal expense against general bookstores for a very small percentage of what they stock rather than against those people who make their living primarily selling pornography, who are, I might add, better able to defend themselves and better able to afford an attorney than the independent book-seller is.

I don't know how many of you know about the book-selling business, it has a small margin of profit. It is hard to make a living by a legitimate bookstore.

I am concerned that if a number of the cases go to Court, it is not likely to help the calendars in Court. I don't know that this has been properly addressed. I am concerned that it appears that written suits need to be about specific books or magazines. What happens if one of these pornography bookstores had thousands of titles, do you have to sue over each title individually? It seems unyielding to me, it seems difficult to enforce.

I have another concern on the Statute of Limitations. To give you an example, the Statute of Limitations on medical malpractice, including assault by a physician, is two years. I do not think that it is appropriate to have a longer Statute of Limitations on the crime of peddling pornography than of the crime of physically assaulting a woman. I was assaulted by a psychologist. When I fought back, I was told by an attorney when I got up enough nerve to sue for malpractice, "Too bad, it was two and a half years ago." You have no cause of action.

I also have some concerns that in addressing movies, again, I don't know, and I wonder, I ask for your, you know, whatever, for your enlightenment, what the effect will be on R-rated movies which I may or may not choose to see, which do run in the downtown houses. There doesn't seem to be any distinction drawn between those and the speciality pornography houses. I am concerned about the lack of distinctions in this legislation.

Finally, I consider this a good start, perhaps meaningless, it seems to me the city has abrogated its police power to forcing women to spend their own money in order to live in safety, in order to keep themselves from being harassed in walking by the places. I have a problem, I like to put the baby in a baby buggy and go down to Sears. I have to pass a number of these places and I am not ready for the harassment outside. The City Council would say, yes, women, we give you the right to get the money to bring suit yourselves, we are not able to do anything for you.

I grew up outside of Boston, I have some questions as to why the combat zone seems to work there. They are under the same constitution as we are, last I heard, and yet for whatever reason it has not been applied here.

And in conclusion, I would like to encourage the committee and the entire council to consider carefully some of these questions I have raised. To consider very carefully the wording in this so when you pass something relating to pornography, and hopefully relating to prostitution as well as pornography, that you will pass something that will have teeth and not force the victims to come up with the money to defend themselves. Thank you.

CHAIRMAN WHITE: Thank you very much.

MS. MacKINNON: Could you stay so you could respond?

You know I may not address everything, you did a lot.

As to what you say, the discriminatory stuff and the things you say would not be covered. The intention of this ordinance is to cover as pornography one, women, because that is where the strongest data is as to the relationship between women in pornography and concrete harms and abuses towards women, but also as to cover as pornography men, children and transsexuals when they are used in the place of women.

MS. STRAUSS: Okay, I think it should be made a little clearer.

MS. MacKINNON: And we accept you saying that it should be a little clearer. In fact I accept that, I will do that.

MS. STRAUSS: Very good, thank you.

MS. MacKINNON: The second question that you made as to the difficulty of the legitimate book-sellers making a living, part of the hope here is that by allowing people to sue, principally women, traffickers in pornography that there will be an alteration in the competitive atmosphere, that is the view. In other words, that women know how hard it is to bring suits that will stick, and we all know who the traffickers of pornography are in the city. And what we are thinking is that it is important that there are not to be exceptions so that pornography can always be available even if because it is only sold in small quantities. In other words, it is just as harmful if you get it at the town grocery store or at a store like yours, if one gets it from there then it is just as harmful in grocery stores as it is if it was bought in an emporium run by the Alexanders.

MS. STRAUSS: I would like to address it briefly, I don't know if you are familiar with the current thing in category romances. Frankly, I find those highly offensive and yet there is a very large — those of us who own stores and make our livings from them would very much like to not have to carry this but there are a large number of women in South Minneapolis who have very little on the way of brain and like this garbage. I can tell you how many we sell.

CHAIRMAN WHITE: This is not a debate, this is a public hearing.

MS STRAUSS: Yes.

CHAIRMAN WHITE: I have initiated your concerns. There has been a response of what?

MS STRAUSS: I am responding to her that we wish we had a guaranteed income, we do have a large number of customers who are regular customers who we can't afford to lose who like this kind of category romance and we can't afford not to carry them.

CHAIRMAN WHITE: We are not going to go into debate, from now on we are going to hear public testimony that will be put in the record and we will not except from the committee members, if they wish to ask a question, but have no responses.

I want to thank you.

MS. STRAUSS: I wish to thank you and I wish to thank those of you who are respectable and those of you who were not, I wish to —

CHAIRMAN WHITE: Let's go on.

Richard Alberta: Some objections

Richard Alberta, you have the floor, three or four minutes.

MR. ALBERTA: Richard Alberta, I live at 4617 East 36th Street. I am a free lance editor for a private journal here in town.

In less than two weeks I have heard three different explanations on the research of pornography and violence. Dr. Elizabeth Rice Allgeier, I sent that testimony to the council last week, said we lack conclusive evidence regarding this issue. Professor MacKinnon said there is a concreteness between exposure and violence. And scientific works on the subject seldom, if ever, use the word causality but rather talk about correlations or results of studies. Which suggests, in other words, different people look at the same data and come up with different conclusions. Today is a perfect time to clear up some of those conflicting conclusions. Now, most of the conflicts deal with words, two words in particular, attitudes and aggression. So, I have organized the conclusions within the scope of these two words.

Number one, aggressive pornography and attitudes. The Malamuth and Donnerstein study of 1982 listed studies regarding this but studies with conflicting results. On the other hand, Malamuth and Check suggested that exposure to films of films showing "aggressive sexuality as having positive consequences tended to increase acceptance of male rape myths". On the other hand another study, Malamuth et al, 1970, found no evidence of changes in attitudes. So one study says yes, another study says no.

On the second and last point, aggressive pornography and aggression, in the laboratory when a female researcher angered a male the aggressive pornography increased his aggression towards her. However, aggressive non-pornographic exposures also increased aggressivity towards female victims.

With regard to the last category of studies, the question has been asked: How do these effects go to outside non-laboratory conditions. Malamuth and Donnerstein, alluded to before, said "While laboratory experiments provide a useful framework for determining whether aggressive pornography can affect aggressive tendencies, there is a need at this point to examine the extent to which such stimuli actually exert and impact in naturalistic settings."

Parenthetically I might add that although we have been told the quality of pornography is increasing and this increase should result in more violence in women, the incidents of rape in Minneapolis have not been increasing since 1973. In fact, in 1981 — between '81 and '82 there was a 7.3 decrease in rape in Minneapolis. So this is a complex issue as well as an emotional issue.

For the benefit of the Council members and audience today, I hope that some of these complexities can be addressed here today.

CHAIRMAN WHITE: Thank you.

Is there anyone that can't be here before 5:00 that wishes to speak? We do have a break scheduled. Is there anyone that can't come at 5:oo and continue the testimony?

MS. MacKINNON: They can and they will be there.

MS. HOYT: Mr. Chairman?

CHAIRMAN WHITE: Yes, Councilman Hoyt?

MS. HOYT: If there is no-one signed up on the list — as long as there is no-one signed on this list who indicated that they can't be here at 5:00, I think the whole audience and the committee might be able to stand the break that we have scheduled. So I would move that we recess until 5:00.

CHAIRMAN WHITE: On the motion, all those in favour say aye.

THE COMMITTEE: Aye.

(Hearing recessed until 5:00 o'clock in the evening on Monday, December 12, 1983.)

SESSION II

CHAIRMAN WHITE: Who will speak here?

MR. BEAVER: I think all of us will.

CHAIRMAN WHITE: Since there are four of you and I notice three on this list, who else?

MR. HYATT: We are also expecting Cliff Greene, he will be in shortly. He is an attorney, he has extensive knowledge in the area of Civil Rights.

MR. BEAVER: And Sharon Warwick may not be on that list that you have in front of you.

CHAIRMAN WHITE: She is not on here.

MS. WARWICK: I was on the other list.

CHAIRMAN WHITE: What other list?

MS. WARWICK: The Civil Rights Commissioner's.

CHAIRMAN WHITE: We need a quorum, will you please come in Councilmember Howard or Daughtery of Dziedzic.

The forum being present, we will reconvene the hearing on the Pornography Ordinance.

MS. HOWARD: Chairman White?

CHAIRMAN WHITE: Councilmember Howard?

MS. HOWARD: I would like to announce, before the public hearing was called a couple of months ago, I agreed to give a speech at the Women Voters Meeting at 7:00. It is not because I am not interested, it is because I can't cancel out on a different speech.

CHAIRMAN WHITE: Okay. We have members of the Civil Rights Commission here who are with us, I am going to allow them to speak briefly with their tentative statements. They will also have an ample opportunity in two days to prepare their concerns or agreements on the ordinance. And at this time, I will allow them to participate.

Whomever wishes to go first.

Tom Beaver, Civil Rights Commission

MR. BEAVER: I am Tom Beaver, Chairman of the Civil Rights Commission. We, as a commission, have not had an opportunity as a commission to fully discuss and talk about this ordinance in a commission meeting. So as of today, we are unable as a commission to give you a yes or no on this issue of our support.

We have some very serious questions. One, how is this going to affect our department and our resources to implement other aspects of the Civil Rights ordinances? And before I can give you a yes or no on the support, we need to have a meeting and we have successfully arranged a meeting between the makers and your consultants, which will take place. And after that meeting we will be making a prepared text to let you know of our support or non-support. It would be unfair to tell you yes or no on our support tonight.

We would like to let you know that we have some concerns and we will talk those out with your consultants and with Charlee Hoyt on Wednesday when we meet with everyone. I sense in the conversations that I have had with other members, the support is not full and complete for this amendment and I think that it might be because of some lack of knowledge on our part on what this amendment is going to do and how it is going to operate.

Until that meeting, until we get our questions answered, we will hold off on formable testimony for you and present it at other hearings. Other members of the commission have things to tell you and some of their concerns, and I will let them go ahead and explain their testimony.

MS. HOYT: Chairman White?

CHAIRMAN WHITE: Councilman Hoyt?

MS. HOYT: I appreciate the fact the Chairman is making it possible for a meeting of the commission to take place. It is my understanding that when our meeting was set up last week with the Executive Director of the Civil Rights Department I made an automatic assumption that also meant the commissioners, and I found out right away that it didn't. And it was hard to call you at 9:00 o'clock and say, would you like to come to a meeting at 10:00 o'clock. I did call Mr. Beaver. It is a misunderstanding on my part, they would have had full access earlier.

CHAIRMAN WHITE: Okay. I would ask you to be as brief as you possibly can because we do have some that have waited over to get whatever they wish into the public hearing setting.

You may go ahead with someone, whoever wished to go.

Sharon Warwick, Commissioner of Minnesotao Commission on Civil Rights

MS. WARWICK: I am Sharon Warwick, Commissioner of Minnesota Commission on Civil Rights. I have a few problems with this. First of all, I would like to say that I am against pornography since over half the proposed zones are in the area where I live and my friends live and where we shop and do business. I am very much concerned with what is going to happen within the city. I am not going to speak to the First Amendment rights, I think there are a lot of other people who can speak to those issues better than I can.

I have a problem with the ordinance and how it is written. I feel it is

44

somewhat discriminatory, particularly with part G which defines the word pornography. I don't believe that it should be exclusive to women. I am also very much concerned about how this ordinance will be enforced and the fact that we will need more staff; concerned about whether or not people realize that it is going to involve a lot more staffing for the department. I think there is a misconception, perhaps, that this ordinance will close the bookstores. I am not sure that that would happen.

I am also concerned about the time that has been spent on this ordinance. As the commission, we have not been approached at all regarding this ordinance and I find that rather troublesome when in fact we are the people who are to be concerned with Civil Rights in the City. And it was almost a surprise when we received the ordinance in the mail. We had naturally read about it in the media but no one had ever contacted us regarding the ordinance itself.

I am not sure that this particular ordinance belongs with Civil Rights. I think that there might be other forums that would deal better with pornography than the Civil Rights Commission. I would like the City Council to consider that carefully.

Again, I am concerned about the time, I hope that we don't rush into something. I think this does need more study and I am concerned that the full council should get time to study all of the testimony that is taken here today. I guess I might like to suggest tabling the matter, if it should come to that point, and give us time to work with it and to talk it over more. Thank you.

Rick Osborne: First Amendment issues

MR. OSBORNE: Mr. Chairman, my name is Rick Osborne, I am also on the Civil Rights Commission. I won't promise to be brief and I hope the Chair will indulge me because you have heard a lot of testimony this afternoon. And I believe that, because this is an issue that is new to the city, having just surfaced publicly some five weeks ago and which potentially involves cost to the city of thousands of dollars to prosecute and enforcement costs, assuming that it is passed and upheld on the part of the Commission, that you will give me a few minutes to discuss with you my concerns.

CHAIRMAN WHITE: Mr. Osborne, I don't want to be capricious, I would like you to limit your remarks to three or four minutes.

MR. OSBORNE: I am on the general speakers' list, if I don't make it now, I will talk then too.

CHAIRMAN WHITE: You are not going to double up on me like that.

MR. OSBORNE: Okay, I will try and make it quick, Mr. Chairman.

I should point out to the Commission that I don't speak on behalf of the Commission; this is my own opinion. The same goes as Assistant Criminal County Attorney in the Criminal Unit and the Appeals Unit.

I have had experience as a counselor for the runaways for victims of pimps. I have some experience and expertise in those fields.

My underlying personal commitment is fighting discrimination against women and all the groups protected in our ordinance. My philosophy is that no matter how noble and good that end is, we must use means to fight and accomplish it that are fair and just and most important, legal. And I don't believe this ordinance meets any of those criteria.

One of the consultants who worked on the preparation of this ordinance said in her introduction today, "The First Amendment is not useful to us." Unfortunately, Mr. Chairman, it is that attitude that has been prevalent on the part of our country's history. Who would deny freedom of speech, freedom of the press, and freedom of religion. The First Amendment was designed to be inconvenient to people who would supress public debate in the country. So, I don't have much sympathy of the drafter because she has that opinion. This committee must not allow legal objections to be ignored by the simple assertion of some that the hearing is merely to find facts. I have specific objections to the proposal itself. First, semantic objections.

The phrase "graphically depicted" is legally meaningless and this is a dilemma that you as a committee have to recognize in that language. I feel that phrase is so overbroad so that the following articles will be banned because they are sexually explicit and subordinate women. I am going to use a definition of sexually explicit as something on a person's face that refers to their sex. Subordinate refers to a lesser position, either physically or power. And graphically depicted merely means expressed or obvious. If that very admittedly broad definition is used, it could be used to cause the following to be banned.

MS. HOYT: One second, be aware that it is simply not that paragraph. It is that paragraph plus one of the nine references that follows it. So in the ordinance, it would not apply if it were simply the one without the others.

MR. OSBORNE: I understand that but that is the initial threshold requirement. The matter must meet that definition before it can consider the others.

MS. HOYT: It has to have one of the other nine with it.

MR. OSBORNE: I understand that.

MS. HOYT: It can't stand alone.

MR. OSBORNE: I understand. With that understanding I suggest that is — it is possible that somebody can try and bring an action against the Commission for the following materials. From Geoffrey Chaucer, *The Wife of Bath's Tale,* "He took his wife in his arms and kissed her, overcome with joy. Thereafter she obeyed him in everything that might add to his bliss, and thus they lived for the rest of their lives in perfect happiness." It is sexual, it refers to her as a wife, as a woman, that is explicit. It obviously refers to her explicit capacity. She is definitely subordinate. Bear in mind it refers to the woman being subordinate because she has to obey the man and which of the other nine criteria does it need? By someone's definition that she is being treated as an object, a thing, or a commodity, it might mean that she is being presented in a posture of sexual submission because we don't know what he meant, Geoffrey Chaucer means, when she is overcome with joy. The problem is, we don't know if that material is going to be covered by this ordinance. That is taking a broad definition.

What if you narrowly define "sexually explicit subordination of women" as: it has to display genitalia or some sexual act, as we understand it. Then I would suggest that the following material, which is objectionable to me and I am sure many of the people that are backing the ordinance, would not be banned. First, the cover of *Hustler* magazine which shows a pair of presumably women's legs in a meat grinder: this would not be banned because there is no display of sexual genitalia. We don't know if those legs are women. The album cover with the women's black and blue body of bruises would not be covered, as I understand it, there was no show of sexual acts and —

CHAIRMAN WHITE: Let me say this. First of all, as I asked earlier on, this is not a debate and your comments, whether you agree or disagree, is not necessary. This is input, this is going into a document, this is very serious business. He is stating an objection to it, possible objection. There will be those that will speak in the affirmative for what has been stated that he objects to. Let us not get into a hair-raising aspect here, this is not a circus. We will let everyone say what they have to say and get it over with.

Go ahead.

MR. OSBSORNE: Finally, I would suggest that if a narrow definition of that phrase is adopted, that any item in which the woman is physically above, especially a man in the process of committing a sex act, would be bannable under the ordinance. I don't think that is desirable. Because I also have here, and I will give it to the committee, a photograph which appears in this week's article of *Newsweek* magazine. It is a classical statue in which breasts of the woman are displayed and genitalia of the man are displayed. The man is physically in the position of pre-eminence over the woman in this statue and I suggest that that would be banned and I don't think that this committee wants to get into the position of doing that. I would submit this to the committee for whatever weight you want to give it.

Now, the whole problem with the definition being vague is from the merchants' point of view. You heard from a young woman who runs a legitimate bookstore. She has materials she didn't know would be covered or not. The merchant is faced with a choice: either he or she has to guess that a book or magazine that is being sold in that bookstore is going to fit the broad definition and therefore get rid of it, or they can take the risk that it would not fit a narrow definition and sell it, and run the risk of prosecution. It is exactly that choice that a merchant has to make.

The First Amendment is designed to protect that chilling effect of uncertainty because a rational prudent business person is not going to carry the item and it won't be available.

I have one final legal objection to this, Mr. Chairman, and that is that this particular ordinance just plain is not needed. We have civil remedies for the victims of assault in the form of court actions for assault and battery. If someone, such as Ms. Marchiano was, appears in movies and she doesn't want to be in movies, she can bring an action in defamation of character or privacies. We have nuisance laws that govern a business that harasses passers-by. They can be shut down if we have the will to enforce them. They are on the books.

We have zoning laws, which doesn't get rid of pornography. To begin with, at least you will allow the First Amendment to come into effect. There are criminal statutes, my office prosecutes sexual assaults. One of my most — one is when I prosecute sex offenders, they are hideous crimes. We can use the laws on the books to take care of them.

Thank you, Mr. Chairman.

MS. HOYT: I appreciate your concerns. Perhaps if we added the word genitalia we could make it so that it is definite. I hope you will take some advantage of being able to press that in the meeting that you are all going to have, to find out if it does. And I plan, if at all possible, I plan to be there.

I caution you one thing, that is: almost every past civil rights ordinance that I have seen has had people in opposition saying the laws were already on the books that could be used.

I can appreciate your concern. I would not want to have culture accused of being pornographic and I believe you will have an opportunity to probe that in depth.

And again, my personal apologies, it was my ignorance of not knowing that the Civil Rights Commission should be there when the Director was, or you would have had that opportunity prior to public hearing time.

MR. OSBORNE: Councilmember, I appreciate that. I guess my position would be, even if the definition is drafted more narrowly, I, as a commission member who will be sitting on at the complaint hearings for this, don't want to be in the position of a community-hearing censor. It is impossible for any of us, no matter how far it is drafted to separate out what is bannable and what is art. The Supreme Court has consistently said that.

CHAIRMAN WHITE: This is strictly for a public hearing.

Ms. Laurence?

Wanda Laurence: effects of concentrating porn in one area

MS. LAURENCE: My name is Wanda Laurence, I am with the Civil Rights Commission. I am speaking on my personal opinion and I am kind of uncomfortable with testifying because of the fact that I have a very close friend that was raped. And the man said, when he admitted the fact that he did rape this friend of mine, that he had just come from a pornographic movie. And I am giving this testimony as my own personal opinion, not necessarily the views of the Commissioner or anybody else in my neighbourhood or the audience.

I live in a neighbourhood that is very, very much inundated with bookstores and theatres that show porno movies or which is usually advertised as porno movies or porno books. Because of the fact that I sit on the Commission, I feel like I have a right to testify just as much as you people do. Also because of the fact that I am on the Commission, I want to make sure that the way it is written, the ordinance, something is written that will not be challenging in court. That it will ban or greatly reduce the amount of pornography that is happening not only in my neighbourhood but in other areas, because I really feel that it not only adversely affects and attacks and dramatizes the life of a woman, it affects youth, it affects men, it affects everybody in some way or another. It affects a person regardless of age. There is a lot of child pornography, there is a lot of pornography that affects women, and I think the majority right now that I have been made aware of that has been what people complained about is the fact that it affects women more than it affects most of the other people. Right now I tend to agree with that. But I find a problem with reading this thing as to whether we can implement it monetarywise. I think that the way it is presently written, it will be challenged in court by the people that have a lot of money to be able to afford to take it into court. And a lot of it adversely affects whether we have been attacked or not. And I think that adversely affects us, this porno stuff, and most of us I daresay in this room can't afford financially to take anybody to court that shows this kind of stuff, sells this kind of stuff or whatever. We just can't afford it. Grass-roots people especially can't afford it.

Most of these places are located in areas that are in grass roots or places where a lot of grass roots people go. It happens to be that that is where most of the people have put these things and allowed a license to occur. Most of these places are in the neighbourhood that I live in and I am really, really opposed to them being there. First Amendment right or any other amendment right, I am opposed to them being there.

I know it is adversely affecting my neighbours who are renting. I speak for a lot of people in my neighbourhood, they can rent a lot of the facilities there because of the fact that there is so much porno in our area. People are afraid of being hassled when they are waiting for the bus and a lot of places where they are waiting for a bus is right outside of these places. I really, really, resent that the bus stop is there. For those that want to patronize the place, if they want to patronize the place that is fine. I resent them being in my neighbourhood, a good share of them.

Also I am opposed to the fact that Charlee she explained, but people were calling me and asking me my views as to how the Civil Rights Commission would handle this type of a thing when I hadn't even received a copy of it yet. I just want to voice my frustration with that.

And as far as the ordinance, I would like not only to see some form to ban this, and especially the effects that is has about women, I would like to see an ordinance change occur where these all aren't located in one area. And from what I have been told, they are going to be located in either downtown or else in commercial areas. And I live not too far from Lake Street which means we would probably get more than we already have. I don't know where they are going to put it, I am afraid that every time someone vacates they are going to put it there.

One of the people that lives next door to me recently said that she —
CHAIRMAN WHITE: Can you wind it up?

MS. LAURENCE: One of the people that lives next door to me said that her sister was raped and that they recently arrested the person that did it. I live not too far from where this person that committed the crime lives. It is getting so that I am afraid, and a lot of people that I have talked to from various parts of the city are afraid to even go out at night.

I believe the way it is written now, some form has to be drafted up, written, that can pass without a phenomenal court battle, that will not only help women so they can feel safe out there but help other people that have put up with this pornography stuff.

CHAIRMAN WHITE: Okay.

Clifford Greene: Drafting and enforcement issues

MR. GREENE: Members of the Council, my name is Clifford Greene, I am in my second term as a Civil Rights Commissioner. I will try and be as brief. I understand the Chairman does not want to get into a great deal of substantive debate. I will merely raise the concerns that entered my mind upon reviewing this ordinance when I did receive it. I appreciate Commissioner Hoyt's comments that the exclusion of input from the Civil Rights Commission was not intentional. I look forward to meeting with the officers of the ordinance, I think we might have some constructive input for all of you later in the week.

I am an attorney and I represent municipalities other than the City of Minneapolis, and have drafted and interpreted local obscenity laws. I am also an adjunct professor of law and teach a Civil Rights course at William Mitchell, serving as a full-time law professor there two years ago.

I make my comments mindful of the evils of obscenity and pornography and also the concern about the need to balance the First Amendment rights. As an individual member of the Commission, my concerns are primarily that I would be asked to adjudicate disputes that exist in coming under this discrimination ordinance. I am very, very careful, as are all of the members of the Commission, to apply the law in a consistent manner so people know what the standards are.

As I read the ordinance, the standards are not self-explanatory to me. I look forward to talking with Professor MacKinnon and her colleagues regarding attention of the drafters of the ordinance, so perhaps we might be able to find some language that would give those who have to adjudicate these disputes, as well as people subject to them, an indication exactly what the standards of liability would be.

I give an example of the concern I have, without resolving it here, we can discuss it later: that is a situation where there is a book containing a character where there is a prostitute, and for one reason or another, enjoys being so. The prostitute character may or may not reflect the opinion of the author that prostitution is good, bad, or indifferent but may in fact be a character in the book to generate thought about a particular issue, perhaps even the issue of discrimination against women in our society. I am concerned that I will be asked to interpret the intent of the author: is the character truly expressing an idea or attitude towards women that is harmful and discriminatory? So I am concerned about how to deal with that kind of problem and troubled by the possibility that I may be asked to construe these kinds of dilemmas. And I ask for guidance from the authors of the bill regarding what they had in mind.

In addition I do have some questions about whether or not the standards as written are constitutional. As currently written my impression, and I state only an impression because I do not purport to be an expert on obscenity, is that they probably are not but they might become so. And I would be very interested in hearing the strategies that Professor MacKinnon has in mind for defending those particular ordinances from the attacks that will inevitably occur. They will occur if the attackers are successful, they will get attorney fees under the Civil Rights Act. Therefore I think we should anticipate a costly battle but be ready to defend one in case it occurs. In particular, my concern is about how the regulation of pornography will enable us to reach types of expression that is not considered obscene under Federal definitions of obscenity.

The courts have allowed us to regulate obscenity, to ban it, criminalize it, zone it, whatever. It is my understanding, and perhaps I misunderstand, that the intent of this legislation is to allow us to create a cause of action for expression that may not be obscene but is harmful because it is pornographic. I would like to understand how this particular approach to the regulation of pornography would be constitutional whereas other approaches to widening the definition of obscenity are not.

I am concerned also about the impact of this proposal on the current operations and objectives of the current Civil Rights Commission. We have been very busy, we take our mandate seriously to make sure that all citizens of the City of Minneapolis have an opportunity to raise their concerns, be they legitimate conflicts, perceived conflicts, or whatever regarding discrimination in housing and in a variety of other activities.

I want to know what the impact of our involvement as a commission will be on other very important activities such as our efforts to assure affirmative action and our efforts to assure that housing is made available to all and that none of the protected classes receives any less attention because of our ability to now deal with the new issue.

Another concern that I would like to discuss with the authors of the legislation is why this legislation is aimed at the local level. I am aware and have previously assembled the multitude of obscenity laws that are enacted by the Federal and State authorities and that are on the books. I wonder whether the intentions of this legislation is to say these agencies will not enforce those laws or saying that these laws are inadequate. It seems to me that there are some tremendous advantages to forcing obscenity laws via State and Federal legislation because they can cross jurisdictional lines. They can deal with issues such as the making of pornographic movies which may not be made in our particular city.

And finally, I would like to understand what the supporters of the legislation hope this legislation will accomplish. It is very important that we not create unrealistic expectations. If the purpose of this particular legislation is to assure that we do not have certain types of pornography exhibited or made available to children or others, I would like to understand that. If the purpose, however, is the expectation that this ordinance will do away with adult, I use the term loosely, bookstores, I think that expectation is unfounded.

I think that fortunately or unfortunately, depending on what your reading pleasure may be, that the adult bookstores are not going to be closed by this ordinance. We are required item by item to take a look at particular materials.

So these are the five concerns that I have, that I hope we have a chance to discuss. And I know I for one will attempt to be as helpful and as receptive and as willing to learn this area as I will be willing to contribute.

MS. HOYT: Mr. Chairman?

CHAIRMAN WHITE: Alderman Hoyt?

MS. HOYT: I will leave most of those for when you have the meeting. However, being one of the major authors I will tell you it is in Minneapolis for the same reason that we seem to have had a sexual preference which is not at State or other levels. It is here not at the choice of the consultants we have hired, but at the request of the committee who in an open public hearing was considering a zoning ordinance on bookstores.

Her testimony concerns Civil Rights of women and at that point the committee requested our City Attorney to talk with the people that we have now hired as our consultants, to help us construct that ordinance. So, it is in Minneapolis at the choice of Minneapolis and at the choice of this committee which said we would like to pursue this and look into it.

I am sure you can go into more depth when you get into your meeting specifically, but do be aware someone did not bring this other than this committee asked for it, and we fortunately have some consultants around.

CHAIRMAN WHITE: I would like to hitchike on what Councilmember Hoyt has said. That is the reason it is before this committee. In zoning and planning they came in with the possible zoning in various aspects of the city, leaving out some. There was a cry throughout the best part of the cities that had those points or sites designated as being the recipient of pornography.

One of the things that everyone here has to understand, the victims are crying out, "What about us?" whether it is burglary or whether it is rape, whether it is any kind of acts that violates the human aspects of our society, they are saying, "What about us" and what they are asking is justice for all.

MR OSBORNE: Chairman White, in my case I missed a point that I wanted to bring to the Council's attention. Many of the underlying sentiments that I am hearing on behalf of the proponents of this proposal are that the attitudes that are infused in our culture, that men have perpetuated violence against women, I don't disagree with that at all. What I would draw to the Committee's attention is that the same sort of attitudes of silence and hatred and empathy have been fused in our culture against gay and lesbian people as well. I don't want the source of that

52

hatred propaganda by evangelists, I don't want that banned by the marketplace either. I want the Committee to know that.

CHAIRMAN WHITE: Okay, thank you. We will now continue with the — would you take your conversations in the hallway, if necessary.

We are going to take this yellow sheet, it only has a few more on it. I will allow them three minutes and then we will go to the proposed sheet of those that wish to speak.

So would you give your name?

Tim Campbell: objections as a gay man

MR. CAMPBELL: Thank you, Mr. Chairman. My name is Tim Campbell, I am here to testify today as a member of the gay male community. I believe that that should be significant to the public and to the City Council and to the Commission as they consider this type of ordinance is that the gay male community has been systematically a target for sexual assault as women have been.

I testify today as a gay rights activist who sat in a cell block for 14 days with four rapists in this very building. I have been the victim of sexual assault three times at the hands of men and once at the hands of women. There is a sexist bias that says the act of violence perpetrated against men is not sexual assault. I beg to differ with that sexist thinking.

In the course of 12 years working full-time as a counselor, a comforter, a theoretician and an activist, for 12 years we have worked from the theory that what is going on at the University of Minnesota is the most effective cure for sexual ignorance and for the violence that results from sexual repression, sexual frustration and sexual ignorance.

As much as I empathize with Linda Lovelace, I believe that this ordinance will be more dangerous than helpful to Linda Lovelace and her kind. Linda Marchiano, victimized under the name of Linda Lovelace, came to the name of freedom under the name of Linda Marchiano and a new body of language.

Basically you heard a lot of testimony this afternoon that amounts to telling you that things lose shock value after you repeat them a number of times. I am here to tell you any drag queen could have told you that. Sure, the more times you see a rape on TV, the less shock value it will have. That doesn't prove anything.

Basically we agree on goals. I would like to see queer-bashing stopped, I would like to see sexual assault against women stopped. I fear, however, this ordinance will only increase the amount of weirdo pornography coming out from the makers.

In the last 12 years there has been a change in the production of gay pornography. In early 1970 it was difficult to find anything but really sleazy, shoddy-looking models and a whole lot of abusive stuff in gay male pornography. With the movement towards liberation and greater access and larger market, normal adult males consenting in adult sex, there is more of it than there was in 1970.

In the recent couple of years a negative reaction to the current drive against pornography, violence in pornography, have what I consider an artificial production of we will show you thumb and nose type of pornography like the cover of *Hustler* that shows the woman going through the meat grinder, or the woman's legs going through the meat grinder. I believe that is temporary. I have great confidence in the long run that as you heard today, these women want to use this ordinance to stop things like the sexuality seminars that are going through and Bart testified that is what she would like to stop, that is what she testified. She objected that medical students were seeing things they called pornography.

I can't tell what will be pornography by reading the ordinance proposed. I can assure you I can find four paragraphs in the ordinance to bring suit against the Bible. Cinderella is a myth that would not pass the test; in fact, I define — I invite the City Council members to sit down now and write a three-sentence story involving a woman and sex that would pass the test of this ordinance. I don't think you would be able to write anything.

So I would ask you one, I believe that this ordinance as proposed is a threat to the Civil Rights. Others pointed out that it is blatantly sexist. It is un-American, it is fascist, it is antisexual and it is antiheterosexual.

Basically, the missionary position is no longer acceptable story telling, the only thing you can do is Jack met Jill, maybe, and neither one pursued the other one and they lived happily ever after is the only love story you could write now. I would ask the Council to send it back and put this kind of litigation somewhere else, don't erode the concept of Civil Rights with this concept.

Robert Halfhill: harassment of gay men

MR. HALFHILL: My name is Robert Halfhill and I live at 125 Oak Grove, Apartment 45. I am opposed to the ordinance also as a gay activist. I will comment first on the ordinance

It states that pornography shall include the sexually explicit subordination of women, graphically depicted, whether in words or in pictures in conjunction with one or more of the following. And then one is, women are presented as sexual objects, things or commodities. That might seem to be a very narrow definition, as came out of this hearing today. It turns out that even though members of this antipornography movement will deny that they are against erotica, when it actually comes down to examples, anything that is sexually explicit is viewing women as sexual objects, or commodities, and so forth.

We had someone testify to the calendars of nude males coming out, she also said gay pornography is offensive to her and she also referred to romance novels which some people might consider pornography. Just the fact that one or more of the following would mean that this ordinance would cover anything sexually explicit.

But I am more concerned with the following: this movement against pornography bookstores has had a terrible effect on the gay community.

There have been three thousand arrests, according to the Twin Cities readers of gay and adult bookstores, under the liberal administration. And every time we go in to talk and complain to the police chief about it, he says I am getting it from the other side.

So the point I am making is that this movement against the bookstores has been one of the factors, perhaps not the only one, one of the factors that led to the arrest of three thousand gay men with the police brutality and insult of police and so forth. One example, we had one police officer, and this will have to be a sexually explicit quote, we had a police officer beat a gay up and he said, "You mother fucking faggot, if I ever see you around here again they will find you in the river and your own mother won't be able to recognize you." What I am here to announce publicly, if this movement doesn't stop the arrest of gay men, we are going to have to retaliate in some way. It is just as easy for us to picket the pornography on U of M Campus as it is for women to picket pornographic bookstores. If it doesn't stop, that is what we are going to have to do.

MS. HOYT: Mr. Chairman?

CHAIRMAN WHITE: Councilmember Hoyt?

MS. HOYT: Could I first reiterate to the audience one of the best things we have in our society is the right of people to testify before their government and make their feelings known. No one should be put down for expressing their thoughts and their views before this committee, and I would appreciate it if we could honor that.

Eugene Conway: pornography and obscenity

MR. CONWAY: I am Eugene Conway, Senior. I am the State President of Morality in Media in Minnesota, Incorporated. We are the state affiliate of the National Organization of Morality Media. I had to leave early and I just got back and I don't know a lot of the things that have transpired.

But our organization is the organization that brought out the minority report of the Presidential Commission and also that was taken in the place of the majority report. Our State organization is 100 percent in favor of this ordinance. We have a few questions about the problems that might come up later on with regard to the constitutionality of the ordinance, but we are generally — in fact, we are in favor of the ordinance.

Sitting here this afternoon, one thing I would like to bring out, we have a long legal constitutional history of obscenity and pornography in this country. In 1957 the Roth decision of the Supreme Court stated very categorically that obscenity is not free speech. Now, this is aimed not only at women but men and every person in society. Those of you that are active in this movement also know that in 1973 the Miller decision of the Supreme Court gave us about seven or eight activities that may be obscene.

The other point I would like to bring out, it was mentioned several times, is we don't have a definition of obscenity. For those of you that follow this closely, I am sure you know the three-prong test of obscenity that was brought out in the Roth decision and reaffirmed again in the Miller decision. Obscenities are actions, words, or shows, depictions, descriptions of activities, from the Roth and reaffirmed by the Miller decision, which would, taken as a whole, appeal to the interest in sex. This is the first standard, the first-prong test of obscenity.

The second is that the obscene activities, whatever they might be, must be patently offensive, as we know meaning very evident that way. One of the justices didn't know how to define it but I know it when I see it.

The third-prong test is that taken as a whole that these activities must lack those four famous values, literary value, artistic value, political value, and scientific value. We also know from Roth and Miller that none of us in ourselves can decide what is obscene, that must be done by our peers in a — by a jury from the jurisdiction.

I would also like to point out one other fact which is very heartening. That was recently, two months ago the President set up a coordinator, Mr. Boch, to co-ordinate customs in the FBI and post offices in enforcing all our Federal laws.

I would like to, as a citizen, maybe ask one question, maybe to Mr. Hyatt or to Professor MacKinnon. We have had a lot of experience in this area. How do you feel that ordinance can cope with the City ordinance, the interpretation of Miller through the Wilke decision and the Supreme Court decision, how do you feel your ordinance will relate to these? Thank you.

CHAIRMAN WHITE: Mr. Hyatt, you can do that in a written answer.

MS. MacKINNON: I will be happy to do that.

CHAIRMAN WHITE: Okay.

Theresa McDermott: Women should participate

MS. McDERMOTT: My name is Theresa McDermott, M-c-D-e-r-m-o-t-t. I live downtown Minneapolis.

CHAIRMAN WHITE: Three minutes, please.

MS. McDERMOTT: All right. I am a peace activist. I think these hearings were very revealing today for the state of our society. We have a Civil Rights Commission that didn't take the trouble to come to this morning's hearings that were upon a very serious matter. They say they have so many other things to do. We are 51 percent of the population, you have rape, abduction, imprisonment, the maiming of women. If that isn't bad enough, the pollution of the minds of the men of our society. What is this society going to come to when they can't see the differences between pornography and a love story, between erotica, nudity, sexuality, and by far deviant behaviour which is punishing us because we don't have the political power to fight you.

How many women sit in the Senate of the United States? How many women ever have? We are 51 percent of the population, I will repeat once more. We are now talking of the possibility of a black man being President of the United States. Black men, I suppose since blacks are 10 percent of the population, are five percent.

We as 51 percent of the population are sick and tired of walking down the street and seeing our names and our faces and our bodies defamed and depicted in this way. The title on your little piece of paper for your citizens to see says "Government Operations Committee." We want to be a part of the government and we want to have some right to define what we are.

The definitions made in literature, as someone pointed out, some 10 or 15 years ago in special politics, if you haven't read it I suggest you do. The way we are defined is, as in literature, it is everywhere and done all by men. Just in the last 10 or 15 years have we had the ability to do it ourselves.

We want the filthy bookstores out. We want the freedom to walk in the streets. We brought you men into our lives and every one of you has a mother and a daughter and a sister, and where would you be without us. We don't do it to you and we demand that you stop doing it to us.

CHAIRMAN WHITE: The Chair would like, I notice that the hands were pointing this way and the Chair, being a male person, I would like to let everyone know that I haven't participated in that kind of activities that you wish to abolish. And I also want to say I recognize the fact that over the years in the history of this United States that the course of Civil Rights is very difficult to come by. There are now cries that are coming from women of color saying, what about us? So you better recognize that those that are the majority of women, that women of color are beginning to say "What about us?"

Go ahead.

MR. DZIEDZIC: I would like to say, starting January 2nd or 3rd, whatever date Council takes effect, there will be seven women on the Council which is majority.

MS. HOYT: Mr. Chairman?

CHAIRMAN WHITE: Yes, go ahead, Alderman Hoyt.

MS. HOYT: I would like to point out that we all recognize that this is strictly not male/female division in society, that there are many, many men who definitely do support the equal rights of women and the recognition of their civil rights.

Paul Price: objections

MR. PRICE: My name is Paul Price. I live at 2707 Garfield Avenue South and I will speak very briefly.

I have a loosely informed background, however I think one that is personally well thought-out and rather conscious. I find that in particular in the list of nine points whereby this proposed ordinance action accusing pornography and the violation of civil rights, in particular number one, is very ambiguous and I think it can be easily substantiated through any discussion you have on a very well practical level as to the definition of those terms. And I fear, because of the ambiguity, as other speakers have mentioned, the possibility of great harassment due to a very wide reception of just what it takes to be a negative sexual object. And thus, you must then be concerned with the recipients of that type of

57

harassment.

I am trying very hard to be an artist and I would find myself somewhat ill at ease with the selection of material that may come to my mind. I think that relates also the points that Dr. Donnerstein earlier this afternoon was addressing and describing, his research concerning the crux of his studies, using as he defined it, sexually explicit aggressive pornography and that concerning activity between consenting adults. I don't find as he strove for I believe in his research, he set that distinction forward, I don't find that forwardness here. With clarity, as one of the members on the Civil Rights Commission addressed, the clarity of the chilling effects.

I would also like to inquire, as it is my very uninformed understanding of the laws in society. It is my belief there are activities that humans involve themselves with in varying levels of abuse, in varying levels of the way their behaviour affects other people. I think in following the logic of this, I as a resident living next door to a bar or a liquor store, might legitimately follow the points of this ordinance and ask that the City Council provide for me the means to sue the purveyor of some alcoholic beverage as their drunken behaviour somehow violated my Civil Rights. I would like to inquire, this is part of what I think or how the area will begin to broaden itself out and I would hope that will be addressed because I think statistically even a stronger case could be put forward as the presence of alcohol in our society is on a much more destructive force as I think most everyone in the psych, therapy could let you know. With the presence of automobiles, all are activities which do indeed violate people's Civil Rights in pursuit of happiness.

Thank you very much.

MR. ROCKENSTEIN: Mr. Chairman, there is a dramshop act where a person who has been served too much alcohol and they hit you and the owner of and purveyor of the goods can be sued. It is a good analogy in this case.

Steve Carlson: evidence is moving

MR. CARLSON: My name is Steve Carlson, I am from Minneapolis. I am not a member of the gay community, but I sympathize and wish to protect the people and Civil Rights is the gay community. I have often said that.

I am very sorry to see the conflict that politics are generating. I hope that we can overcome that here. I will not appeal to any interest or hatred for one class of people against another, justly or injustly because I understand, and I am not preaching, but I understand that love is the most powerful force which is operating in this society right now. I hope that it is operating right here in this room today. It hurts me to see all this hatred.

I was here this afternoon. What I saw moved me very deeply, as I am sure it did everybody in this room. I have no doubt that at this time everybody in this room wants very much to stop the kind of activity which we were advised of. I have no doubt that we all want to work together to use the law to further the sanctity of human life. And I don't mean any religious or ideological overtones by saying that, I mean it very simply it is not cool, it is not in any way hip going around beating off, mutilating women, or subjecting them to this. And anybody who starts talking about the First Amendment and being glad that it allows the feeling that somehow it is proper protection, I believe they do not understand the law.

Let me get to the point, the point is we have a job to do. I am proud to be here in this room with these people, and these people who I am very glad to meet and I hope I can align myself with.

The lawyer over here, the one on the end of the Civil Rights Commission, brought up some very helpful input as well as did the person from the media on morality. There has been a lot of progress as we have learned today and know already on obscenity. We should proceed on the local level. We should proceed immediately to protect the life and well-being of the women and others when they are victims of pornography. We should act as far as we can within what the law has already provided. Protections against obscenity, you can even ban it. Obviously that we have come this far today, it shows we are mindful of protecting that.

The new area that has come up today is violence against women. We must — we had a psychologist who presented new painful but startling and protective research and some findings. I wish that all of us would act together to put into effect what we have come to know through this research, through the advent of women's studies at the University which indicates a great deal of hope in this process, in this society, to be concerned about and appreciate the contributions of women's rights. It has brought to us its knowledge. We must extend beyond the obscenity into the evidence. We have to protect property, personal well-being of women, and that is why I hope that we will get down to work. I thank you.

CHAIRMAN WHITE: Now we have some requests of personal testimony that has been on the agenda for quite some time and I would like to allow those persons who are about to begin to speak, to utilize their three minutes and move on. If there is any questions from the committee, I would hope you would hold it brief.

They will be excused from giving their address because of some of the degradation that they have suffered. And we don't want you to know where they live and so forth and so on.

So if the first person to speak is here, Ms. H?

MS. DWORKIN: Mr. Chairman, the people who are going to speak to the actual ways in which pornography has been against them would very much appreciate being able to sit up here.

Ms. H: experience of rape involving pornography

MS. H: My name is -- and I live in the 9th Ward, I am going to talk about being raped and how pornography was involved in that rape.

MS. HOYT: Could you pull it a little closer?

MS. H: When I was 13 I was camping with the Girl Scouts in Northern Wisconsin. It was 10 years ago in November. I was walking through the forest outside of the camp in midafternoon and came upon three deer hunters who were reading magazines and talking and joking around.

I turned to walk away and one of the men yelled, "There is a live one." And I thought they meant a deer and so I ducked and tried to run away. I realized that there wasn't any deer in sight and that they meant me. And I started running and they ran away — they ran after me. I tripped, the forest was covered with pine needles and leaves and they caught me. And I told them that I would go away, to leave me alone, please.

And they said, "You are not going anywhere" and forced me to get up and pulled my hair and started looking at me up and down, calling me a little Godiva, I had long hair then, a golden girl, and making jokes.

They told me to take my clothes off and I did, it was very cold, it was November. I took my clothes off and they told me to lie down and the first man started — they told me not to say anything, that if I made a sound that they would kill me, they would blow my head off.

MS. MacKINNON: Were they armed?

MS. H: Yes. All three of them had hunting rifles. They, two men held their guns at my head and the first man hit my breast with his rifle and they continued to laugh.

And the first man raped me and when he was finished, they started making jokes about how I was a virgin and I didn't know how they knew I was a virgin but they did. And they made jokes about this and jokes about how they could use something like this when they were in boot camp and made jokes about being in the military.

The second man raped me, none of the men attempted to kiss me or touch my breasts, they simply wanted to have intercourse. When the second man was finished, the third man was not able to get an erection and they, the other men, told me to give him a blow job and I didn't know what a blow job was.

The third man forced his penis into my mouth and told me to do it and I didn't know how to do it, I did not know what I was supposed to be doing. He started swearing at me and calling me a bitch and a slut and that I better do it right and that I wasn't even trying. Then he started getting very angry and one of the men pulled the trigger on his gun so I tried harder.

Then when he had an erection, he raped me. They continued to make jokes about how lucky they were to have found me when they did and make jokes about being a virgin. They started kicking leaves and pine needles on me and kicking me and told me that if I wanted more, that I could come back the next day.

Then they started walking away and I put my clothes back on and it was not far from where they had set up their camp and I looked down and saw that they had been reading pornographic magazines. They were magazines with nude women on the covers.

I went back to the camp — well, first I got my clothes back on and walked a fair amount away and then I broke down and cried under a tree and decided what I needed to do. And I went back to the camp and I didn't tell anyone that I had been raped. I went to the bathroom and saw that I had bled on my underwear so I assumed that I had gotten my period. I did not know that virgins bleed. I didn't find that out until a few years later.

I didn't seek any medical help, I didn't tell anyone that I was raped until I was 20 years old.

MS. DWORKIN: Had you seen pornography before?

MS. H: Yes.

MS. DWORKIN: Could you say how?

MS. H: My father and my older brothers all had pornography, they kept it under their mattresses and under their beds. I had looked at the pornography that was in my home when I was growing up. When I was a young child I assumed that that is how it would look when I grew up.

MS. DWORKIN: So you recognized the magazines as being basically the same kinds of magazines that you had seen in your home?

MS. H: Absolutely.

MS. MacKINNON: What do you remember about what you were thinking they would do to you at the time?

MS. H: When I was being raped, I thought they were going to kill me. I assumed I wasn't going to live through that, that this was what they were going to do to me before they killed me.

MR. HYATT: Excuse me, what went through your mind when you decided not to report this?

MS. H: Well, in retrospect I realized that I felt like I needed some control over what had just happened, that I didn't feel like I could tolerate anyone and having them think it was my fault or blaming me or not understanding. And to have no control over who had that information once I told someone, knowing that my mother would most likely tell a great deal of people and I would have no control over that information.

MS. MacKINNON: We are finished.

CHAIRMAN WHITE: Okay, thank you. I recognize that was difficult with all the ears that were here, for you to sit here and make that kind of statement, thank you.

I will probably say this to them all, it takes a lot of guts.

Ms. B: experiences of coercion

MS. B: I live in the 10th Ward.

CHAIRMAN WHITE: Will you bring the mike up?

MS. B: Okay.

I am afraid to be here. I am also afraid not to be here. In thinking about coming here today to speak, I realized that my life would be in danger. As a woman of color these dangers seem many and great, an absolute loss of credibility and respect, wrath and disgust, potential violence both verbal and physical, and ridicule and harassment to name a few. I also realized the dangers to my life if I did not come. These dangers being complacency, letting go of my rage and terror about pornography and its impact on my life, accepting that the shame is mine, accepting that I am the slut and the whore that deserved what was done to me, believing that I am useable. I have no illusions about men not seeing me as a slut, they do. They see all women as sex itself, even the ones they venerate. But I also want to say to you that I have no illusions about my refusal to accept that I am and must always be these things.

I want to tell you how pornography has affected my life, how I am fighting self-loathing, disgust and shame, how I am fighting at the beginning, and how I am fighting tearing out my skin.

The first thing I want to talk about happened when I was three years old. When I was three I was sexually abused by a 14-year-old neighbor boy. I would tell you it seems really bizarre to me to use the word "boy" because the only memory I have of this person is as a three-year old. And as a three-year old he seemed like a really big man.

I was told by him and some other neighborhood kids, which also included his sisters, that we would be playing a secret game. They told me that it was safe and they had played it before and that I had nothing to be afraid of.

What this game consisted of was each child going into a tool shed with this guy. When my turn came I didn't want to go in because I was scared, it was dark in there and it was dirty. There were cobwebs and there was this giant pitchfork.

One of the kids pushed me inside and shut the door. Then this boy grabbed me and he pulled down my shorts and sexually abused me. In short, he finger-fucked me and made me masturbate him. I was really terrified. I thought I was in hell, and I was also in a lot of pain. I started crying really hard and he finally let me go, but I was told that if I told anyone I wouldn't be believed, that it was all my fault and that I would be punished. He also told me that he would hurt me again if I told anyone.

His sister told me that this game he had learned from dirty books. I knew that he had these dirty books because I had seen him with them.

The second incident I want to talk about occurred eight years ago and I want you to know that for the past several weeks I have been living in hell because for the first time I am remembering this. And for me this memory is my first experience with it.

About eight years ago I went to a friend of mine's house for dinner. She was living with what I call her pimp friend, most people would call him her boy friend. Some male friends of hers — of theirs came by and she went out to the store to get something that they had forgotten for dinner. While she was gone someone poured me some wine and after she came back I drank it. She came back, I started feeling really dizzy and disconnected and I wanted to go home. They kept telling me to stay, that I could sleep there, everyone was laughing at me. I found out later that I had been drugged.

What I remember is this: I am on the couch and everyone is looking at me, laughing. They are talking about me — they started talking about taking pictures of me. I am not sure they took pictures; I passed out. I do remember flashing lights and what I do know is that they made and they

62

sold pornography.

What I remember next is being on the stage of this club where my friend strips. I want you to know that I use this term "friend" not with a lot of sincerity. I knew it was this club where she stripped because I had been there before, I had tried previously to understand and to accept what it was she was doing and so I had gone there with her and her parents.

I remember being on the stage and there were two men that were holding me up and they were taking my clothes off. A third man was sexually fondling me. I saw lot of faces in the audience that were laughing and men were waving money, one of them shoved it in my stomach and essentially punched me. I kept wondering how it was possible that they couldn't see that I didn't want to be there, that I wasn't there willingly.

I am not sure what else happened. I have real bad feelings about what may have happened. Somehow, I don't know how I got to a pay phone and I called this friend of mine who came and took me home.

You are probably wondering have I told anyone about this, as to the incident with my friend, no, I didn't report it to the police. How do you report something you don't remember, even when you remember; if you are a woman, even if you do remember you are not believed. Even if you have bruises, you are bleeding, or whatever. I didn't remember anything and what could I have reported?

And I didn't tell anyone about the sexual abuse when I was three because I was terrified and I was real ashamed. And also because I didn't have the words to describe it, I didn't tell anyone about that for 24 years. I confronted my friend about the incident, and she told me that it was all my imagination. I told her I didn't have an imagination and I was trying to find one, she laughed. I asked her why I had been found naked, passed out by the phone if it wasn't true and she told me that was a joke.

Like I said before, I don't know if any of those men fucked me, I do know that that boy fucked me. I know that in both instances I was violated and I am not alone in these experiences.

There are thousands of women and girls who are forced and coerced into accommodating men's degrading sexual pleasures.

Now, you tell me that pornography doesn't hurt women, doesn't violate us, does not use and abuse us, does not instigate and inspire the abuse of women. And when I say women, I include children, in particular girls. I don't understand how anyone can believe it is harmless, I don't understand how anyone can call this fantasy, a deflection of aggression against women, I don't understand how anyone can say that this is speech when actual live women are being brutalized.

On the other hand, I can understand it because it is men who are saying this. It is the pornographers who create it, who get the money from it, who get erections from it and society shuns this. I want to stop this for me, for all women and for all girls. There are men here and we have heard from some of them who say that pornography has to exist because they have a right to it, its pleasure, its so-called politcal message. I disagree and I want you to consider this when you make your decision about these amendments. At what cost does this have to exist? Surely not at all costs, surely not at the cost of any woman or girl's life and integrity.

I am going to urge you for once to look at pornography for what it really is, a violation of women's civil rights and I want you to take action to stop it.

CHAIRMAN WHITE: Thank you Ms. B.

Ms. R: sex affected by use of pornography

MS. R: My name is -- and I live in Ward 14. I would really like to thank Ms. B for saying what she said.

I am also afraid to be here and afraid not to be here. What brought me here is that I know a lot of women who have stories to tell about how pornography has hurt them and how they are trying to recover from the destruction it has brought into their lives and that can't be here because they are still working through a lot of that pain. This for me is also a way of purging my own shame about this. I would also like to preface what I am going to say by saying that in my testimony here I say "fuck" three times because I believe in calling something what it is.

I was 21 years old at the time. It was 1980, in March or April. I did have a sexual relationship with this man for about a year.

He had gone to a stag party, this particular evening I was home alone in my apartment. He called me on the telephone and he said that he had seen several short pornographic films and that he felt very horny. Although he did make some general comments about the content of these films, I do not remember what they were at this time specifically. So he asked if he could come over specifically to have sex with me. I said yes, because at that time I felt obligated as a girl friend to satisy him. I also felt that the refusal would be indicative of sexual quote unquote hang-ups on my part and that I was not quote unquote liberal enough.

When he arrived, he informed me that the other men at the party were envious that he had a girl friend to fuck. They wanted to fuck too after watching the pornography. He informed me of this as he was taking his coat off.

He then took off the rest of his clothes and had me perform fellatio on him. I did not do this of my own volition. He put his genitals in my face and he said "Take it all". Then he fucked me on the couch in the living room, all this took about five minutes. And when he was finished he dressed and went back to the party. I felt ashamed and numb and I also felt very used.

This encounter differed from others previous, it was much quicker, it was somewhat rougher, and he was not aware of me as a person. There was no foreplay. It is my opinion that his viewing of the pornography served as foreplay for him.

There were no lasting detrimental effects on me from this experience alone. It was simply an intensification of the ordinary treatment I received from him. It is ordinarily something I feel worth noting and this usual treatment did result in feelings of low self-esteem, depression, confusion and a lot of shame.

64

I do not have any knowledge of him purchasing any pornography at any time in the relationship. I know that the friends he got together with twice a week, they had it in their homes. He was exposed to it regularly.

I feel what I have to say here is important because I feel what he did, he went to this party, saw pornography, got an erection, got me to inflict his erection on. There is a direct causal relationship there. Thank you very much.

MR. X: *Pornography and violence in the gay community*

MR. X: My name is --. I live in the 9th Ward. I strongly support the proposed ordinance on pornography. I am going to tell you how pornography affected my life. Obscene is not the word for pornography, pornography is dangerous. I was battered by my first lover, and the pornography each of us used condoned the violence.

When I was younger I was exposed to heterosexual pornography, including *Playboy, Penthouse, Oui,* and other magazines. It was one of the places that I learned about sex and it showed me that sex was violence. When I saw there was a specific relationship between men and women, the woman was to be used, objectified, humiliated, and hurt; the man was in a superior position, a position to be violent. In pornography I learned that what it meant to be sexual with a man or to be loved by a man was to accept his violence. When my lover was violent, I was taught that the violence was normal. I accepted the violence which I did not like, and it was some time before I left the relationship.

My ex-lover used pornography. One of his first contacts with other men were in gay pornography theaters. He used pornographic magazines before I met him. He started wanting to look at pornography together, I believe that the pornography influenced his behavior.

As our relationship progressed, it became violent. He threatened me with a knife, forced sex on me, and battered me on different occasions. The heterosexual pornography that I had been exposed to was one thing that convinced me that this kind of treatment was normal. The battering was one of the most profoundly destructive experiences of my life. Pornography has showed me that a man's love was violent and to be close to my ex-lover I had to accept his violence.

There is a lot of sexual violence in the gay community, and pornography condones it. I was with my ex-lover after he had been raped by a casual sex partner, and my ex said that rape was just a risk you had to take. I was with a friend after he had been violently raped by his boy friend and his boy friend did not understand that violence and force was not supposed to be a part of sex. The objectification and the violent themes in pornography promote and increase these kinds of violence.

I understand pornography to be a force in creating violence in the gay community. I was battered by my ex-lover who used pornography. The pornography, straight and gay, I had been exposed to, helped convince me that I had to accept his violence, and helped keep me in that destructive relationship.

Pornography is harmful and I want something to be done. The proposed ordinance provides concrete measures for action.

MS. A: *acting out pornographic scenes*

MS. A: My name is --. I live in St. Paul. I am here today to share with you some of the ways in which the presence of pornography is directly related to physical, sexual, and psychological abuse in my life.

My first introduction, before I began in the game of art or more directly under the guise of art, my earlier recollection is of my boy friend and he was an art student, we were sitting together, I 17, he 19. He showed me art books and also books, magazines of pornography. And as he was showing me these works, he was doing critique of women's bodies, of their facial expression, of parts of their bodies and of their dress. Following this was a critique of my too athletic, too muscular body. I was 17, it was very devasting to me that my body was being torn apart in this way.

Within a year my boy friend had a photography assignment and he came home from school and asked me if I would help him with his assignment. When I asked him what it was, he said it was a photography assignment where he had to photograph a series of pictures in which he had to use a woman. He said the woman had to be naked and said he thought that I would want to help him do this. When I objected to doing this he told me, he came up with the reply, "You don't want me to see another woman naked, do you? You never know what could happen and I really thought you would want to help me." He said he had the perfect site, it would only take a few minutes.

The next — I was home from school with the German measles at the time. The next day he picked me up, we went to the perfect site, it was an abandoned bus in an overgrown field. When we got there he asked me, he told me to take off my clothes and to pose in various positions, either draped over the corroded, rusty seats or in positions where I acted as if I was running towards the door. And then he asked me to put my body in contorted different positions, draped down the stairs of the bus, and they were quite jagged, and at that moment I realized that we were depicting a murder. I became very terrified and scared and I was really cold. I told him I didn't want to do this and that I wanted to go home and that I was really scared.

While we were doing this, I would like to backtrack for a minute, I wasn't achieving the right facial expressions for the pictures so he started telling me stories that depicted pursuits during rape so that I would have the right expressions on my face like the women in the magazines. I remember being very distant from him and just wanting to get home. I remember being very scared.

When he had his next assignment, this was about a year later, and it was casting bodies in plaster. At the time I told him that I would prefer if he hired models to do this. On one occasion I flew out to see him at college and he said that there were several positions that he couldn't get the models that he was paying to model in, either because the plaster was too heavy or because the women would start fainting. When you put plaster on your body it sets up, it draws the blood to the skin and the more area it covers on your body, the more blood is drawn to your skin. You become dizzy and nauseous and sick to your stomach and finally faint. I tried to explain this to him because I was a pre-med student at the time and he said, "if you would just like to help me with these," he said, you know, "my work is being shown in the current art shows and it would be a good exception and I would like if you could help me create these artistic pieces."

So I told him that I would try. The first few attempts I failed, he was very disappointed. I failed under the weight and under the heat of the plaster. He wanted me to be in poses where I had to hold my hands up over my head and they would be numb and they would fall. He eventually tied my hands over my head. Finally he succeeded, he ended up getting a plaster cast of my body.

MS. MacKINNON: Do you recall if you did faint at that point or not?

MS. A: I remember I was fainting as he was pulling the cast off my body and he said "it is not quite set yet, hold on, see if you can hold onto it for a little longer." At that point I think I had been holding the pose for about 40 minutes.

After this he switched to water colors. At the time when I was 21 I graduated from college, I was thinking about going to medical school and I wasn't receiving a lot of support at that time for that decision. "Women weren't supposed to do that" was the message I was getting.

At that time I married this man and for the next two years we mainly pursued our careers.

During the second year of our marriage he started reading more and more pornography. He started out reading *Playboy* and started picking up magazines like *Penthouse* and *Forum* and as I would come home from dinner — come home from work and fix dinner, he would read excerpts from the magazines. Some of them were articles and some of them were letters to the editor, ranging from group sex, wife swapping, anal intercourse and bondage, to mention a few. I was really repulsed at the things he was reading me and I was really in disbelief. I kept saying "people are just making these things up for this magazine, I don't believe it." He bought more and more magazines to prove to me that people weren't making it up, that all of these people were saying how wonderful these things were.

About this time when we went out we started meeting his friends at wet T-shirt contests, amateur strip nights or elsewhere. We would meet together as a group or pornographic adult theaters or live sex shows. Initially I started arguing that the women on stage looked very devasted like they were disgusted and hated it. I felt devastated and disgusted watching it. I was told by those men if I wasn't as smart as I was and I would be more sexually liberated and more sexy, that I would get along a lot better in the world and that they and a lot of other men would like me more.

About this time I started feeling very terrified. I realized that this wasn't a joke any more, that this was something that he was really serious about. I called my mother and I told her that there were things happening in my marriage around sex that I really didn't like, and she told me that divorce was something that she didn't want in our family and it was very disgraceful and she knew how competent I was and she said, "I know you can hang in there and give it your best."

About this time, to kind of numb myself, I remember that there was a lot more drinking with my husband and I and with our friends. When people would come over to dinner, there was a lot of alcohol consumed, he would bring out a drinking and stripping game. After the game began he started to ask the people to live out the various different scenarios that he had been reading to me in the magazines. A few times the people participated in this. A couple times I stayed, once I left.

Following this we would have incredible arguments with each other. I would tell him I loved him, I only wanted to love him, I wanted to be a good wife, I wanted our marriage to work but I didn't want to be with these other people. It was he I wanted to be with and no one else. He told me if I loved him I would do this. And that, as I could see from the things that he read me in the magazines initially, a lot of times women didn't like it but if I tried it enough I would probably like it and I would learn to like it. And he would read me stories where women learned to like it.

During this time, once when I was asleep at night and a friend of his was over, he asked the friend — he set up with a friend to come into our room and sleep with us. I woke up finding this friend in bed with us. Once he realized that I was not a willing participant in this experience, he apologized to me and said he was sorry and he left.

To prevent more of these group situations, which I found very humiliating and very destructive to my self-esteem and my feeling of self-worth as a person, to prevent these I agreed with him to act out in privacy a lot of those scenarios that he read to me. A lot of them depicting bondage and different sexual acts that I found very humiliating.

About this time when things were getting really terrible and I was feeling suicidal and very worthless as a person, at that time any dreams that I had of a career in medicine were just totally washed away. I could not think of myself any more as a human being.

Because of his job we were transferred overseas. When we got to overseas, the pornography that he was reading and that his friends were reading was much more violent than the pornography that he had been reading to me at home. He started taking me to sex shows where there were women and animals, especially snakes. He started taking me to sex shows where the women were called "banana lady shows". We went to sex shows where men were participating in the sex acts with women on the stage.

About this time he started having to go away a lot and I was left alone. I started studying karate over there and I also started feeling again like I had some kind of control over my body. And I started really feeling in touch with the fact that I was a person. I started traveling, I did a lot of traveling by myself and I started feeling more and more courageous.

I went to the Philippines on one of my last visits overseas and I was there for three weeks. During the time that I was there I was staying mainly at a Navy base. Outside of that navy base the prostitution was very visible and very explicit. Everywhere you went there were men hiring prostitutes, those were the only women that I saw there. I was one of the few American women.

One night when I was in one of the pornographic institutions, I was sitting with a couple of people that I had known, watching the women on stage and watching the different transactions and the sales of the women and the different acts go on, and I realized that my life wasn't any different than these women except that it was done in the name of marriage. I could see how I was being seasoned to the use of pornography and I could see what was coming next. I could see more violence and I could see more humiliation, and I knew at that point I was either going to die from it, I was going to kill myself or I was going to leave. And I was feling strong enough that I left.

I spent the next few years of my life, through the help of therapy, education and friends, healing myself. I would like to forget that the women's story is me but I know those memories and those scars will remain. Pornography is not a fantasy, it was my life, reality. It involved abuse to my body to create it.

If what I said today can help prevent one woman from experiencing what I experienced, the pain that I was involved in, it is worth it. Thank you.

MS. DWORKIN: I would like to ask you just a couple of questions. How old were you when you left marriage?

MS. A: I was 25 when I left and my divorce papers came through when I was 26.

MS. DWORKIN: How old are you now?

MS. A: I am 29

MS. DWORKIN: I just want to ask you about when you were married and when you were still in the States. Did your husband talk to you about making films and making the kinds of things that he was seeing with you as a participant?

MS. A: Yes he did. Both when we would go to the amateur nights, he would try to get me up on stage and I refused to do that and then when he would read through the magazines, one of the things that became a theme for a while in the magazines were husbands trafficking their wives, having sex with a friend or some man. And there would be — I remember various stories, one was about a woman in a cabin and it was all staged how the man would be hiding, how the husband would be hiding to photograph his wife, and he tried to get me to do that several times.

MS. DWORKIN: During this period of time were you actually raped in your marriage?

MS. A: Yes, I was. I actually refer to my whole marriage as marital rape. But specifically at the time, what I was considering rape was several times, especially following the incidents where he asked our friends to

69

come to bed with us after I was already asleep, following that time he felt that it was his privilege to, when I was sleeping, if he felt at all sexually turned on or in the need to be gratified, to rape me in my sleep. Most of the times I would wake up. Sometimes I would just keep my eyes closed and try to tolerate it.

MS. DWORKIN: So this could happen to you any time when you were sleeping?

MS. A: Yes, it could happen to me any time when I was asleep. And several times when I confronted him on this he said if I refused to have him do this then he had to masturbate. And as I know from his religious background, that was a sin.

MS. DWORKIN: When you were actually living in the Orient you said that the porn was very much more violent. Coul you describe to us what was actually in it than what you had seen before?

MS. A: Okay. The pornography had mostly Oriental women in it and black women in it and it depicted women as animals and had women having sex with animals in it. It was women in cages. There were a lot of whips, I guess some of them is what they call S and M pornography. Women were led around with collars, they showed women being penetrated anally, they showed more gang rapes. It was more abusive in that the women were not portrayed as these glamorous perfect women, what I had seen before, they were portrayed more as slaves.

MS. MacKINNON: Could you describe in a couple of words what you see to be the relationship between the pornography and the things that your husband asked you to do?

MS. A: He would read from the pornography like a textbook, like a journal. In fact, when he asked me to be bound, when he finally convinced me to do it, he read in the magazine how to tie the knots and how to bind me in a way that I couldn't get out. And most of the scenes that we — most of the scenes where I had to dress up or go through different fantasies were the exact scenes that he had read in the magazines.

MS. MacKINNON: Did your husband remarry?

MS. A: He remarried within the year that we got divorced to a woman that was almost 10 years younger than he was. And at the time I had seen him to finalize things on our divorce and get some of my last possessions, he showed me pictures of her and said, "Do you want to see what she looks like?" They were pictures of her naked and in pornographic poses.

MS. MacKINNON: Thank you

MS. DWORKIN: Thank you.

CHAIRMAN WHITE: Thank you.

MS. Z: Prostitutes' experience of pornography.

MS. Z: My name is --. I live in the 7th Ward. Before I start, I just want to say what is happening right now is very incredible to me and I know it is very hard for everyone in this room to be here and to be listening to these

70

horror stories. And I hope that people stay with their full concentration for the rest of the evening.

I am speaking for a group of women, we all live in Minneapolis and we all are former prostitutes. All of us feel very strongly about the relationship between pornography and prostitution. Many of us wanted to testify at this hearing but are unable because of the consequences of being identified as a former whore. This is absolutely incredible to me that prostitution is seen as a victimless activity and that many women are rightly terrified of breaking their silence, fearing harassment to themselves and families and loss of their jobs.

We have started to meet together to make sense of the abuse we have experienced in prostitution and how pornography endorses and legitimizes that abuse. These are some of our stories. The following has all happened to real women who are the exception because they have survived both pornography and prostitution. We are living in Minneapolis and all of these events happened in Minneapolis. And as we sit here, this abuse is happening right now in the City tonight.

One of the very first commonalities we discovered as a group, we were all introduced to prostitution through pornography, there were no exceptions in our group, and we were all under 18.

Pornography was our textbook, we learned the tricks of the trade by men exposing us to pornography and us trying to mimic what we saw. I could not stress enough what a huge influence we feel this was. Somehow it was okay. These pictures were real men and women who appeared to be happy consenting adults, engaged in human sexuality.

Before I go on, one might make the assumption that if a women got involved with pornography and prostitution after she was 18, that she is a willing participant. And since the women I speak for were all under age when they began, it is easier to see them as victims.

Personally, I feel this to be very dangerous. By talking to women who got involved with prostitution and pornography in their early 20's, the powerlessness and victimization they described and experienced is the same that younger women and children feel.

Here are specific stories we have shared, about how pornography encouraged and taught us and how it was used to brutalize and terroize us as women.

One of us had the experience of being paid by a client to go to a house located in the 6th Ward. When she got there she found a group of physically disabled men, and a group of physically abled men. Everyone was watching pornographic films. Movies of men fucking women, women doing oral sex on men, and women being penetrated by animals. The movies were played continuously.

The able-bodied men were joking and making comments like, "That's how real men do it," instructing the handicapped men, teasing them that if they watched enough of these movies they would be able to perform normally. There were constant remarks made about what normal male sexual experience was. Then the disabled men were undressed by the able men and the woman was forced to engage sexually with the disabled men,

71

there were two weapons in the room. The woman refused and she was forced, held down by the physically able men. Everyone watched and the movies kept going.

There were various physical deformities, amputees, paraplegics. Some were able to perform, some weren't.

After this, the able-bodied men said they were going to show the handicapped men how "real men" do it. They forced the woman to enact simultaneously with the movie. In the movie at this point a group of men were urinating on a naked woman. All the men in the room were able to perform this task, so they all started urinating on the woman who was now naked. Then the able-bodied men had sex with the woman while the disabled men watched.

Another story is, a woman met a man in a hotel room in the 5th Ward. When she got there she was tied up while sitting on a chair nude. She was gagged and left alone in the dark for what she belived to be an hour. The man returned with two other men. They burned her with cigarettes and attached nipple clips to her breasts. They had many S and M magazines with them and showed her many pictures of women appearing to consent, enjoy, and encourage this abuse. She was held for 12 hours, continuously raped and beaten. She was paid $50 or abour $2.33 per hour.

Men would constantly want to do what they have seen in pornography. If pornography was not actually in the room with the client, there would be constant references. One example is that a woman was in a room with two clients, one man told the other that he had seen some pictures of woman who had shaved their pubic hair and that it had turned him on. They then proceeded with a jackknife to remove the woman's pubic hairs, plucking and burning what the knife missed. They made comments of how her hairless vagina remined them of their young daughters' genitals. They then, of course, engaged in intercourse.

Women were forced constantly to enact specific scenes that men had witnessed in pornography. They would direct women to copy postures and poses of things they had seen in magazines and then they would take their own pictures of the women.

One man paid a woman in the 6th Ward $35 to recruit another woman so he could direct them in a lesbian scenario he had seen in a movie. She was supposed to recruit the other woman for him. When *Deep Throat* was released, we experienced men joking and demanding oral sex.

It is very amazing to me what happens when a group of ex-prostitutes get together in one room and tell stories. One of the things we discovered was that the men we had serviced were very powerful men in this community. Especially interesting to us are the amounts of men involved in the media, in this community, that use prostitutes and pornography. These are the same men that perpetuate the myth that Minneapolis is a clean city with exceptional morals and a high quality of life.

In closing I would like to say that in my experience, there was not one situation where a client was not using pornography while he was using me or that he had not just watched pornography or that it was verbally referred to, and directed me to pornography.

72

I know that this is a very complicated issue. I am asking you to recognize the pure simplicity of it. Men witness the abuse of women in pornography constantly and if they can't engage in that behaviour with their wives, girl friends, or children, they force a whore to do it.

My wish is that you could see with my eyes just for a day how clear the relationship is between pornography and the systematic abuse of women.

I would also like to say that I'm petrified and scared for young women today. I believe the pornography that is published today is more brutal and dangerous than when I was involved. And because I understand clearly the direct relationship between material and the abuse of women, I am terrified of the consequences of what that means. I worry about how this will affect your daughters, who I know will be victims in one way or another to this pornography. I also worry about the prostitutes on the street who are currently being used by the pornographic industry. I know that we are helping them tonight by speaking out and voicing our outrage and by saying that as adults who believe in human rights and human intimacy, that pornography is absolutely not acceptable to us.

The other thing I just need to stress is that every single thing you see in pornography is happening to a real woman right now. There is no way out of the connection and that we are responsible for knowing and having that information.

I also have a couple of written testimonies of women who were not able to speak tonight for the reasons I already give.

This is a story of a woman who works at the University of Minnesota and could not speak for herself. She was involved in prostitution between 1970 and 1974.

"I remember a house on Second Avenue South, near 22nd Street which I was asked to go to by a trick. He told me that I would be able to make a lot of money there. It turned out to be the same house that my pimp had been urging me to go to where he told me young pretty girls could go and get tied up, beaten and burned with cigarettes and earn $500 for a short half hour's work. I had steadily refused to go, but when my pimp found out that I had been invited, so to speak, I had to go there.

"The woman who ran the place actually lived there with her children. She kept a room upstairs for the tricks to use. It had a projector to show porn films and there was stacks of pornographic material in the room. The tricks would go there, look at the porn to get psyched up and then the girl would be sent to the room. The youngest girl I know about who went there was only 13.

"When I went into that room, the trick said that I was almost too old, but he was pleased with me because I looked young. He stripped me, tied me up, spread-eagled on the bed so that I could not move and then began to caress me very gently. Then, when he thought I was relaxed, he squeezed my nipple really hard. I did not react. He held up a porn magazine, with a picture of a beaten woman and said, "I want you to look like that. I want you to hurt." He then began beating me, and when I didn't cry fast enough, he lit a cigarette and held it right above my breast for a long time before he burned me. I told him that as God was my witness, he had better kill me or untie me right now, because if he didn't I would turn him in to the police and that I would call his wife and tell his family about him. He believed me and let me go. But I know that this house continued to provide that service for those who could pay.

"When I worked at massage studios, the owners had subscriptions to *Playboy*, *Penthouse*, *Penthouse Forum* and the like. These magazines were arranged in the waiting area of most of the massage places which I worked in. If a girl was not inside with a trick, she was expected to sit out front with the men who were waiting or who were undecided, and to look at the magazines with them in order to get them titillated. The men would ask me questions like, 'Do you really like it when more than one man fucks you?' 'Do you really like to suck men off, like this hot little number who wrote the letter to the *Forum*?' et cetera. They used the soft porn to help them work up the courage to try the acts described in the magazine with the prostitutes at the massage studio. At one point, I was on the company payrolls of a couple of well-known businesses in Minneapolis. One of these companies, an insurance firm, kept an apartment in Edina which was used as a place to entertain big clients when they came to town. The place was very expensively furnished, had parquet oak floors, a well-stocked bar, and in the closets, stacks of pornographic films and magazines and pictures, as well as lingerie for the women to wear. When I was there, what usually happened was that the man in Minneapolis who was in charge of entertainment would invite some local associates who wanted to have a good time along with any visiting big shots who needed or wanted to be entertained by the apartment. The men would usually get there first, and start drinking and watching porn movies. Then three or four women, always a lesser number than the number of men present, would arrive. They would ask us to get into the lingerie and maybe show another film or bring out pictures. And then the intercourse would start, all in one room, so that some men were watching. This was all straight sex and the men were never coercive, but I got paid extra money if I could find prostitutes who were willing to have anal sex or who were willing to perform oral sex on another woman in front of the men. These slightly deviant acts were depicted in the films and photos in that apartment. Although I don't know one way or the other, I have no reason not to believe that this apartment still exists today."

This is another story of a woman who is currently working downtown in Minneapolis.

"I was the main woman of a pimp who filmed sexual acts almost every night in our home. The dope man, who supplied us with cocaine for free in exchange for these arranged orgies, was a really freaky man who would do anything. They arranged to have women, who I assumed were forced to be there, have sex with dogs and filmed those acts. There were stacks of films all over the house, which my pimp used to blackmail people with.

"One day I came downstairs in time to see a very young girl run naked out of the house. I found her friend, also naked, tied up in the closet. The one who ran away, after being forced to perform sexually all night, went to the police. I don't know what my pimp did with the other girl. I do know that he kidnapped them and felt safe, because they were foreign and alone. The girl came back with the police, but nothing ever happened. My pimp continued to make films of people doing every kind of sex act in the living room of our home. He was never involved in the acts, he got off on watching."

The other things, very briefly, that I need to address tonight, and some other women have addressed it, it is the specific abuse of women of color in our community, specifically black women and the Native American women living here. There is a native woman, C---- L------ who will testify tomorrow night, who six months ago was brutally raped and beaten. And the men that attacked and raped her were making continuous comments about *Custer's Last Stand,* which is a video thing about these men chasing a squaw and they do things to her. They said, "This is better than *Custer's Last Stand,* let's try the chase scene in *Custer's Last Stand.*"

I want people to know that there is pornography dealing with color and that is happening in our community right now.

That is all I have, unless there is questions.

MS. DWORKIN: May I ask you a question? You talked about how all of the women that you were meeting with and talking with were introduced into prostitution somehow with pornography.

MS. Z: Yés.

MS. DWORKIN: Could you describe that a little more and talk about the relationship between the pornography shown and pictures actually taken of the young women that it was being shown to?

MS. Z: How it was introduced was that young women would be picked up on the street, off the street, and everyone's first experience was always the same which was that the man would show either magazines or take you to a movie and then afterwards instruct her to act in the way that the magazines or the films depicted. Usually after, I call it a training period, what would happen then is that these men or different men would set up scenarios of usually more than one woman to very, very specifically copy and reproduce scenes that were portrayed in magazines and books that they had witnessed. And then they would make their own movies using home video equipment and also Polaroid cameras, and they would all collect their own library of pornography involving these women.

MS. DWORKIN: Thank you.

MS. MacKINNON: Thank you.

Discussion on alcohol and drugs

MS. CARLSON: I have a question of Mrs. MacKinnon and some of the people that have talked, and I would like to preface my question by thanking the people that have shared their stories tonight. I know it was extremely painful for them, for me, for the women to share their stories.

The statement is, I have gone through somewhat the catharsis that the women have gone through in my bout of alcoholism. I have shared many of the same things in the first step, in group treatment, and I have heard some references to drinking and use of alcohol and I am presuming the use of drugs in some of these stories.

And my question of you, and I am not going to be able to stay for the rest of the testimony, I have a meeting, but my question to you and the women and men that shared their stories is: how much alcoholism or alcohol and drugs are relevant in the stories?

MS. DWORKIN: Thank you for the question, it is a very, very, good one. The answer is that the abuse of drugs and alcohol is absolutely systematically present through almost all of these stories. And that there is a cynical and purposeful use of both drugs and alcohol by pimps on women, both to produce the material, that is the pornography, and to keep women in prostitution.

MS. CARLSON: My question to you though is one of: could it be the use of chemicals, drugs, or alcohol that has caused some of these problems rather than pornography?

MS. Z: What I know about that is there is a group of Christian men who actually use pornography and prostitutes in this town, and they are totally against the use of alcohol and they manage to do just fine.

MR. DZIEDZIC: I will announce that the next speaker will be -- --, followed by -- --.

MS. MacKINNON: What I would like to also say, Councilman Carlson, is that while the use of drugs and alcohol are part of the systematic pattern of abuse, it isn't the same thing to say that those things cause that abuse. In other words, we are making the argument that pornography motivates it, inspires it, leads people to believe that it is justified, that it makes it profitable, and that it also — it basically defines it as something that is okay to do.

Once it is defined as something that is okay to do, it is okay to abuse these women in these ways, then anything that is abusive to women becomes okay to do and drugs and alcohol are those things.

Do you see what I am saying?

MS. CARLSON: What I am hearing you say is that the pornography is the beginning?

MS DWORKIN: All of these stories that you have heard are representative of a thousand more stories and some of them involve direct drugging. And we are not talking about people, about women who are choosing to drink, although in some cases, for instance the testimony of Ms. A drinking was part of her life style and it was part of being able to endure the abuse.

I think it is important to understand the different situations in which drinking and drugs are used. But the constant in all the situations is the pornography.

MS. MacKINNON: Also, the men are not doing what they are doing to the women because of alcohol and drugs. The data that we had earlier on today showed a direct casual relationship between pornography and aggression towards women.

MS. B: My name is -- --. I talked earlier. What I want to say to you is that what I am hearing is a tendency, and I find that real dangerous, to say that these people were drinking or were on drugs. And so therefore, we attribute it to that and that really frightens me because in my situation I was in a normal social situation, I had gone to dinner. No one was drinking, I was on my second glass of wine as were the other people. Some of them were on their first. What I know is that this was something that was planned and there is no way that any — that I can attribute any of what happened to me to my being drunk or any of these men being drunk because they weren't.

Ms. Q: pornography and sexual harassment

MS. Q: I am -- --. I live in St. Paul right now, I used to be a resident of Minneapolis. I am simply going to relate what happened to me about four years ago on the job. I, for the past six years, have been in training as a plumber. And about four years ago I got stuck on a job that was almost completed but not quite. I don't know if you understand construction set-ups, but generally in the winter, certain trades will get together and have a little shack inside of a building where they will eat lunch and have coffee and everything else.

When I got on the job, three of the trades has set up a nice little shack and had lunch there. And it was a real shock when I walked in, because three of the four walls in the room were completely decorated with pictures out of various magazines, *Hustler, Playboy, Penthouse, Oui,* all of those. Some of them I would have considered regular pinups but some of them were very, very, explicit, showing women with their legs spread wide and men and women performing sex acts and women in bondage. It was very uncomfortable for me to go down there and have dinner and lunch with about 20 men, and here is me facing all these pictures and hearing all these men talking about all the wonderful things they did on the weekend with all of these women.

I put up with it for about a week and it finally got to the point where I could no longer tolerate sitting there and realizing that all of these men were there, I felt totally naked in front of these men. The only thing they talked about during lunch period was women, their old ladies, their girl friends, and all their conquests of the weekend.

I got to the point where I couldn't put up with it any more. And being one of the only two women on the job and being rather new at it and not knowing that I had any alternatives, I got pissed off one day and ripped all the pictures off the wall. Well, it turned out to be a real unpopular move to do. I came back in at lunch time and half the pictures were back up again, they pulled them out of boxes and stuck them on the wall and proceeded to call me names. And just basically call me names and otherwise ignore me.

MS. MacKINNON: Do you recall what names they called you?

MS. Q: There was one electrician that had it in for me, he always said, "Hey, bitch" or some other term that didn't really sit with me too well. It was very, very hostile.

So after lunch I went back in and took them all down again and I came back the next morning and some of them were back up again. At that point I decided that I no longer wanted to eat with these men and I began to eat my lunch at other places in the building and was totally boycotted at work. The men wouldn't talk to me, I mean I was treated like I had just done something terrible.

Just by happenstance, on that weekend I was at a meeting and was relating my story to some women and one of them happened to be a woman who worked for the Affirmative Rights Office in Minneapolis. She said "We can help you out," it was an affirmative action job, it was getting Federal funds. And she organized three other women and herself to make an unannounced inspection and they did that. And I said I don't want them to know that I had anything to do with this because I am scared. And they came and took note of all the pictures that were up, I hadn't tampered with them any more, they were all on the walls. They wrote letters to each of the companies involved.

And during this time, at some point when I was at work, this one electrician was extremely angry at me. I have no proof that this man did this but I came out of work one day, my car door was bashed in. It wasn't parked anywhere near where any other car would have hit it, it was bashed in in a place that wasn't logical to be hit by another car. I have no proof that this man did it but I had a sneaky suspicion on that. He was removed from the job, subsequently.

After the LEAP Offices and State had written letters to send out to these various employers, my boss, the man who owned the company, called me up one day and said, "Look, I heard you are having a little trouble down there, why don't you just kind of calm down a little bit. Don't make such a mess. We don't need any trouble down there, just calm down, just ignore it." I said, "Hey, I can't ignore it. I don't have to, I can't, it is already done." A couple of days later they got the letter and they were told that this did not comply with the action guidelines. In the meantime, I had asked for a transfer and my transfer came through which was very fortunate but —

MS. MacKINNON: What part of your transfer did this pornography play?

MS. Q: It came a lot faster is what happened. They decided I was making too much trouble and had to get me out of there.

MS. MacKINNON: Was it where you wanted to transfer to?

MS. Q: No. I had requested that much earlier and had been waiting on it. But it was really uncomfortable, I felt no support from the men, none of the men at all. In fact I approached my boss one time and said, "I don't like these things," and he said, "I can't do anything about it, these men do what they want to do." And I said, "Piss on it, I will do what I want to do."

It would have been nice if I would have known that there was some action I could have taken, knowing that I didn't want those pictures there or not knowing that I could have taken them down. Shots of women's genitals.

MS. MacKINNON: Do you have any idea, just to enlighten it for all of us, what their stake in it was, why they kept putting it up over and over?

MS. Q: I, for a long time, and you know this might not be right, but this has been my sense, I mean I have encountered pretty much hostility in the last six years being the only woman on the job doing men's work. On that particular job I was a legal threat because I had replaced one of the other men who was causing trouble, who was one of the good old boys and I think they were doubly angry at me on that job and they wanted to get rid of me.

CHAIRMAN WHITE: I think we will now take a short recess, be back in 10 minutes.

(Short recess.)

CHAIRMAN WHITE: We will resume the public hearing. There is a time certain at 9:00 o'clock. If there are people who have added their names since the last time, I don't know who came up and got this, but they have added their names, so I would like the people to utilize the three minutes because the other persons that testified gave stories of their lives that were rather horrendous and we gave them a little more than the time that should have been allotted. But we are after 8:00 o'clock now so we will move right along.

Ms. Y: intimidation in a pornography district

We have -- --. Did I say that correctly?

MS. Y: I won't correct you. I prefer to have it said the way it was, that is fine.

I am a resident of St. Paul and I have been throughout the majority of my life. What I would like to provide you first is a personal history of where I have been.

I have lived in St. Paul the majority of my life, excluding five years. And during those five years, it was more than five years, it was eight years. During four years of which I went to the University of Minnesota in Duluth and the remaining four years I lived in Toronto, Ontario in Canada. What I learned during those eight years was very difficult, I was away from St. Paul, I knew my city very well before I went to the University of Minnesota, Duluth. And when I came back from Canada in 1978 I felt I still knew my city, even though I was away from St. Paul.

My husband and me moved close to Dale Street and University which is located close to quite a lot of pornography places: the Faust Theater, the Flick and the other is called the Belmont Club. I remember when I was a little girl on Sunday we would drive by the Belmont Club, I would say "What is the Belmont Club?" and my father would say "It is nothing that would interest you, S------." And still being a young girl, I didn't care much if my dad said you are not concerned.

What happened, I went to the local high school, I went to St. Agnes High School which is located only four blocks from those three pornography shops. And at that time the Faust Theater and the Flick were not in operation so the Belmont was still a pretty silent place, and everyone who lived in that neighborhood felt rather protected and secure from being subjected to sexual harassment and violence as a result of pornography.

What happened is that my husband and I moved into the residence in 1981 and at that time I was exposed to sexual harassment that I never knew existed. What I would like to discuss are three of the types of sexual harassments that I had to face within two years. For myself it was disgusting, it was very frightening, and I really don't think that I have any way to work around it and that's the strongest fear that I have at this point.

I would like to speak on behalf of the other people who live in my residence because we all, to a large degree, feel that we are invisible, silent people. Our neighborhood is very working class, a lot of people don't have 9:00 to 5:00 jobs. They are working in the afternoon or afternoon shifts. We are the type of people who like to have our voices heard, we don't have political power, we don't have money, we are barely making it day to day. When it comes to having people hear us speak, we don't feel we are heard. The police that are working in neighborhood are upset with the Faust and the Flick because a man can pay a quarter and go and see a quarter show, and all he has to do is pay two dollars and he can have a female completely nude to do all the dancing for him in three minutes.

The police have gone to the Flick and tried to bust it, time and time again. Finally the police in our residence have said "Forget it, we are giving up, nothing has been done. We are not going in there and taking the chance of having our heads blown off." Us, the people that live in the neighborhood, we have to fear that day in and day out, especially the women.

Just last week I had an exceptionally horrifying situation when my husband was not home and a man tried to get into my house by both the front and the back door. He wouldn't leave, he continued to knock, he was trying to get the door open. And it was so serious in the sense that the police even tried to get him but at the same time too, they didn't make the attempt. What this boils down to is that the police have come to the end of the rope with my neighborhood. They feel that they can only do so much and consequently, they are not giving the same protection and same security which they did for other neighborhoods. I empathize with them, there are a number of good people that don't live in our residence but happen to be at porno shops and they subject the police to constant harassment. They subject them to the fear of physical abuse and consequently, the police are in a position where they are stepping back. But the people who are paying the price are myself and my neighbors.

What I said before was that within two years I had been subjected to sexual harassment. It all started in 1981 when I moved — my husband and I moved in. At that time I was pregnant and I was walking to the Country Club Store across the street but I was in the vicinity of the Belmont Club, the Faust and the Flick, and a middle-aged man, white, he had on a business suit, was crossing the street same as myself. Right off he asked me if I was a prostitute. We were crossing University Avenue. I was shocked, I wanted to get away from him as fast as I could but at the same
80

time I was seven months pregnant and I couldn't run, the best I could do is walk and ignore the man. I came home and I was shaking like a leaf with my husband. He was so disgusted, because there was not a damn thing he could do. He has to hope to hell that his wife is going to be able to live a somewhat normal life.

Then it happened again where I was going to Wendy's Hamburger Shop, instead of asking me if I was a prostitute, he asked me how much I cost. You are just in a position when you think, when is this going to stop? Is it because I live close to these pornography shops that this continues to happen?

The third time that it did happen to me, I am very firmly convinced that it has a very strong significant high correlation with the pornography. The third time it was another work — another business man but at this time the man was around the age of 50. Rather than ask me if I was a prostitute or how much I cost, he walked right up to me and said, "You are the dancer from the Belmont, aren't you? I saw you a couple of nights ago, you really did a good job." You don't know what to say. I am in that position where I am so thoroughly frightened. I am shaking in my shoes. At the same time I am so disgusted, I would like to be able to tell him how I feel. I can't do that, especially living so close. My fear is that this man is going to be very disgusted with my comment and he can follow me right home.

I have a daughter who is two years old and there are many mothers, many parents who live in my neigborhood. The average number of children per block on my block is at least 15 kids, and those I am referring to are infants all the way through to 18-year old children. And we all have to face that constant fear. What is it going to be like when my daughter is old enough that she can walk and go to the stores? How often can I tell her, "Don't go there, that is a bad place for you to go". All the parents feel that way but at the same time we feel powerless. We don't feel that we have the voice and we don't feel that people will listen to us because we are working class. It is a very sad situation.

The last thing that happened to me puts me in a position. I have epilepsy, I have a physical disability whereby I am partially conscious during the seizures. As a result of that, I can look very quote unquote normal in the sense that I hear a person to a certain extent but I can't comprehend what the person is saying to me. I can see things but that doesn't mean I am going to be able to do the correct thing in the sense of seeing a green light and walking with a green light. I might see the light but go ahead and walk, even if it is yellow or red.

The last time it happened I was in the bus shelter, it was raining and I decided I was going to take my chance and sit there rather than being wet and going to work. As a result of that two men saw me, this is — everything occurred during the daylight, nothing has happened at night which is more difficult to deal with. In the evening I can't even walk out of my house. With this happening during the day, a man came on one side of the bus shelter and a man on the other side. I was inside. They came into the shelter at the same time and talked to me as if they had known me. I didn't know who the men were. And automatically I have that fear — I was in front of the Belmont Club — that these men are going to interpret me as being a prostitute or a dancer and it boiled down to them asking me if I was a prostitute. With it happening three times before and one more time, I just got to the point where I was going to try my chance and shock these men as best as I could, and I played as if I was mentally retarded. It was a sad case to go through, they both saw me as being the person I am now.

I totally ignored them, I didn't respond to anything they were saying. They continued talking and finally one of them said "Do you happen to know what the time is?" It's just crazy, the only thing I could do was say, "Well, I really don't have a watch on now but I think it is about 11:00 o'clock." (Using slurred speech.) It frightened the men, it put goose bumps on me because I think "This is what I have to do in my own neighborhood to protect myself." And these men walked away from me. They didn't want any contact with me at all because I played the role of a woman who was mentally retarded.

It is a sad case when the police have approached my neighbors and myself and they said, "The best recourse you have and your husband have and your children is to get up and move." Why should I have to move from my neighborhood when this is all I can afford? This is the very best type of structure that my husband and I ever are going to gain. At the same time the police are at the point where they are ready to give up. At the same time they are explaining to us, "We really empathize for you but get up and get out, that is your best result, that is your best recourse." And that is why I wanted to come tonight because I know the concept of pornography is associated with the First Amendment in regards to freedom of speech.

In my life nothing compares to the freedom of equality, the freedom of not feeling fear and being sexually harassed, the possibility of being sexually raped, the possibility of sexual abuse in another form of rape. I would give my freedom of speech up in two seconds flat if I knew myself, as well as my daughter, as well as my husband and all my neighbors, didn't have to face the garbage that results from the Faust, the Flick and the Belmont Club.

That is why I hope everyone that is here tonight will take a strong look at this. I have invited many people who have supported pornography to come to my neighborhood and live there for a week and I will walk you all past the Belmont Club, Faust, and Flick. I will give you a tour, you can see what it is like, you can bring your children and bring your wife and anybody else who supports pornography. You move into my neighborhood and I will move into yours. It chokes me up because you have the power, I don't.

I have worked with cases of women who have been sexually harassed. I have worked with young mothers who are single, as a result of rape. They have children physically handicapped because of it. The children are going to have to grow up facing the result that they are a by-product of rape. These young women who were exposed to pornography from day one, they are accustomed with all the pornography magazines, *Hustler* is nothing to them. The *Playboy* is like *Time* and *Newsweek,* they are so adjusted to this psychologically because it's been rammed down their throats. They have had no alternatives.

And all of you have a very strong say in what can happen in Minneapolis as well as St. Paul and I really hope you do something about it. It has got to stop, there has got to be a time where a woman as well as a father can have the opportunity to say, hey, we live in America. We have the opportunity to be treated just as equal as everyone else, unaware of money, and unaware of status and accreditation. Everyone should be treated equal. I would like to end there, thank you very much.

CHAIRMAN WHITE: Thank you for coming from our sister city, it just goes to show it is not just one block or one street.

MS. MacKINNON: I believe that Steve Jevning is going to speak for the neighborhood group.

MR. DZIEDZIC: Chairman White?

CHAIRMAN WHITE: Yes, Councilman Dziedzic?

MR. DZIEDZIC: I was disappointed to hear that the police told someone in the neighborhood to move. That is really a poor indication on whether or not the police can control a situation in a neigborhood. I am sorry to hear that goes on in St. Paul. I think we could put a stop to that kind of rhetoric in Minneapolis.

Whenever you hear that, the way to answer is to tell the police officers that their hands aren't tied and they have every right to enforce the laws to make that a safer neighborhood. If they don't, their boss should come and see the Council and there should be steps taken. I am not talking about just this issue. When a police officer tells you that, he is saying he can't do his job is what he is saying.

Steve Jevning, Neighborhood Pornography Task Force

MR. JEVNING: Mr. Dziedzic, Mr. Chairman, Members of the Committee, my name is Steve Jevning. I represent the Neighborhood Pornography Task Force. The Task Force is really the most recent organized group of a number of concerned citizens in South Central Minneapolis who have rallied around the issue of fighting pornography for a number of years. The Task Force members are for the most part made up of residents of the Powderhorn Park and several neighborhoods of Central Minneapolis who happen to have a number of adult entertainment establishments within their city-designated boundaries.

I would like to start my comments tonight, and I will indeed keep them brief, by telling all of you that I feel privileged as a white, Anglo-Saxon Protestant to exercise my First Amendment right to speak in favor of the proposed Civil Rights Amendment that would guarantee Fourteenth Amendment rights for all members of this community, particularly women who are under-represented at the least, and abused, raped and killed at the worst. I have spoken before this Council Committee and other committees of the City Council about the need for the City of

Minneapolis to take steps that would indicate not only to the women, the men and the children of this community how important they are in the eyes of political leaders, community leaders, but also to take a step that would indicate to this society as a whole that in at least one tiny city, village, whatever, there are people, men and women elected to represent their constituents who are committed to support the rights of everyone. To exist day to day in this society with reduced levels of anxiety, fear, so that they too can feel as comfortable and as privileged as I do as a white Anglo-Saxon Protestant male, to do the things that they should all be able to do, to live a peaceful life, to live an important life, and to contribute in ways that make this society a better place to live for this generation, for the people who are here today, for the people who are yet unborn so that one day people can look back upon the actions that this Council will hopefully take and say that here was a group of people who identified an overlooked problem, and overlooked ill of society. But they realized the significance of that tiny overlooked problem as being extremely representative of the overriding inequities that exist, continue to exist, and in fact flourish today.

Pornography is a very graphic representation of the sexual inequalities and the conflicts between power and powerlessness that exist in this city and this state and in this country. And I urge you to put aside some of the questions which you are finding difficult to answer and take a bold step and allow the answers to be formulated by those people who are not as courageous as you have been. Thank you.

CHAIRMAN WHITE: The Chair would like to say this to you, -----. It does my heart good to hear a younger person talking about the comraderie amongst people, whether he is white, Anglo-Saxon, Protestant or if he is Afro-American or whatever, but as a human being, because this did exist here in this city, and there are those of you that know that, and people did not lock their doors, women were not afraid to walk the streets, the crime that we have in our communities that transcends all of the things that we talked about here today did not exist here in this city as rapidly as it is today. And hopefully what you are saying is that with the help of all others, we can buy us a society back as much as possible, reach into the past and bring forth that which is good and make it applicable and do it again in our society and today and in the future.

Statement by Women Against Pornography

MS. MacKINNON: Chairman White, might I be able to be permitted to read a letter which is written by Women Against Pornography, which is the foremost group working against pornography in this country. I think it will give a national perspective to everything that was stated here locally. I would appreciate the permission for me to read this letter. I think it will take two minutes.

CHAIRMAN WHITE: Two minutes.

MS. MacKINNON: All right. "Dear Councilmembers: The steering committee of Women Against Pornography would like to convey to the

Minneapolis City Council its strong support for the proposed amendment to Title 7, which would enable women to sue persons trafficking in pornography. We believe that this amendment is urgently needed, and we call upon the members of the Minneapolis City Council to support its passage.

"Women Against Pornography is a New York City-based feminist organization with a national membership of 7,000 women and men. We believe that pornography perpetuates a system in which women are regarded as subhuman beings who seek out and deserve humiliation, ridicule and abuse. Since our inception in 1979 we have been fighting pornography through a diverse program of education and activism. We have held public forums, lectured at over 500 high schools and colleges, organized boycotts, and sponsored demonstrations and marches. Although we have made considerable progress in raising public consciousness about the misogynistic and sexually violent nature of pornography and have had tangible victories stopping sexually degrading ad campaigns, we have met with little success in our attempt to curb the growth and the abuses of the pornography industry. Our fight against that industry makes David's battle with Goliath seem like a contest between equals: the feminist anti-pornography movement, composed largely of volunteers and funded primarily by individual donations, is up against a seven-billion-dollar-a-year industry with roots in both respectable corporations and organized crime.

"Although our work has not curbed the power and influence of the pornography industry, it has made us acutely aware of the magnitude and severity of the harm done to girls and women by pornography. We have received phone calls from women who have been sexually abused by men who used pornography as the script for their assaults. We have received calls and letters from women whose employers and co-workers have used pornography to harass and intimidate them. We have heard from wives whose husbands have pressured them to act out their favorite pornographic scenarios. Our storefront office in the Times Square pornography district has been visited by women who reported being coerced to perform degrading public sex acts in order to keep their jobs in a nearby pornography emporium. We organized a speakout in which dozens of women testified about the ways in which pornography has impaired their sense of self, self-esteem, sexuality, and relationships. (The tapes of this event are herewith.) Recently, we received a phone call from a mother whose 14-year old daughter was being recruited for *Hustler* magazine's "Beaver Hunt" by a pair of 14-year old boys emulating *Hustler* publisher Larry Flynt. (A letter from the boys to the girl is attached.)

"We have learned that women are hurt by pornography and hurt badly. Up to this point, however, there has been nothing we could do to help women victimized by pornography take action against those who victimized them. The proposed amendment to Title 7 would provide us with the means to help these women receive justice. It would be a tremendous step toward ensuring that women are regarded and treated as citizens equal to men, deserving of the same civil rights and human dignity.

"Our organization has long been reluctant to endorse laws against pornography because most such legislation has been written in terms of obscenity and has thus failed to address the real harm caused by pornography — its physical, psychological and social injury to women. In addition, we have been concerned that legislation against obscenity might be used to censor women and members of other oppressed groups. We have also declined to support zoning laws, which usually are designed to protect property values rather than the rights and welfare of women. The only piece of legislation we have endorsed has been a section of New York State's penal law that prohibited the production, distribution, and/or display of certain clearly specified sexual performances by a child under 16, without couching the prohibition in terms of obscenity. (This law was first struck down by the New York Court of Appeals and later upheld unanimously by the United States Supreme Court.)

"Because the proposed amendment to Title 7 is directed not against obscenity but against discrimination on the basis of sex and because it is concerned neither with "prurient interests" nor with property values but instead with the abuse and subordination of women, we feel confident in giving our whole-hearted support. Moreover, because the amendment's definition of pornography is so specific and narrow and because it so accurately describes the pornography we have seen, we believe that it could not be applied to material other than pornography.

"We understand that legislation like the proposed amendment would not end our work or the need for feminist groups fighting pornography. Advertising images, which are saturated with pornographic values, would not be affected by this ordinance. Nevertheless, we are convinced that this legislation will equip us with an invaluable new tool with which to challenge the practice of the pornographers.

"For more information about our organization's analysis of pornography, see the script to our slide show (attached). Key passages are marked in blue ink.

"In closing, we would like to express our gratitude to the Minneapolis City Council for developing and supporting this ground breaking legislation. Such support indicates a rare commitment to the rights and welfare of women. We hope that the Minneapolis City Council and this proposed amendment will serve as models for city and state governments throughout the country. Sincerely yours, the entire steering committee."

MS. DWORKIN: Mr. Chairman, I am not going to try to read a whole letter —

CHAIRMAN WHITE: Wait a minute, no. Some of the Council members are going to have to go and if you can submit that letter, these people have got their names here and it is getting close to 9:00 o'clock. We will try and get as many of you as we can. If we don't reach you at 9:00 o'clock, then hopefully you can come back tomorrow at 5:00 o'clock, please do that.

MR. DZIEDZIC: Mr. Chairman, I am sorry I couldn't attend the whole meeting this afternoon. We had an intergovernmental meeting and we had a press conference on the "I" Team. Right now at the Government Center, across the street, there is a hearing going on with problems in Northeast Minneapolis, I will have to excuse myself and go over there. There are three events planned tomorrow evening and all of those events start at 5:00 o'clock. I will come tomorrow and stay as long as I can. I would like to know the intention on what the time frame is on the vote from you.

CHAIRMAN WHITE: The intent of the time frame?

MR. DZIEDZIC: Yes.

CHAIRMAN WHITE: Hopefully at the end of the public hearing tomorrow we can take a vote.

MR. DZIEDZIC: I was wondering about the objection from the Civil Rights Commission that we table this to look at the ordinance.

MS. HOYT: We will have had their letter by Friday so if it goes the other way, that can be taken into consideration.

MR. DZIEDZIC: I will repeat my intent to not have it go to Council on Friday, that the Civil Rights Commission be given the opportunity to look at it, repair any damage that was done with them as far as this body not going through the proper channels. I have heard a lot of testimony today, I have been sensitized by what I have heard. I can recall issues in the past, I have heard issues in the past and recall becoming sensitized with the events as they occurred. With color breaking into baseball in 1948, having witnessed different singular schools become co-educational, one of them being the college I attended. And I remember a letter that I received from that college that was asking for input from alumni. And I wrote back: with a wife and three daughters, you figure out how I would have voted or what my input would be as it relates changing St. Thomas College to co-educational college.

I think the main thrust of the ordinance, I think we are going to have some difficulty as Alderman Rockenstein said today, this is probably the first day of a 10-year battle. Like our fight for civil rights is still going on.

I think that the basis of what we are trying to do is have some input. I don't think you are talking about just pornography, I think you are talking about the whole printed media and some of them which have been legitimized, *Playboy* and some of those magazines, have some of the best ratings. I think that when you — please don't be a high school audience.

UNIDENTIFIED SPEAKER: Don't be a high school speaker. Are you testifying, sir?

Is he testifying? You are wasting time.

CHAIRMAN WHITE: It is all right, he is on the Committee.

MR. DZIEDZIC: I think the whole motion picture industry will have some sort of fight of what we are trying to do here. I think all of those things should be taken into consideration. That is why I think we shouldn't vote on Friday.

There have been nasty people out there today, I will tell you right to your face.

UNIDENTIFIED SPEAKER: It takes one to know one.

CHAIRMAN WHITE: Would you go ahead.

Ms. E : child abuse recalled by pornography

MS. E: My name is --. I live in the 6th Ward. I am not going to speak about the ordinance, I am going to speak about my life also.

I was at the demonstration on Lake Street and Chicago Avenue a week and ago along with a number of other women who went into the porn shop and movie theater there. I looked, glancing really at the images on the shelves and on the screen and even in the midst of the large and angry powerful group of women, I was afraid.

Two days later, having failed my attempts to keep these images away from me, I was sexually abused in my family. I don't know if the man that abused me uses pornography but looking at the women in those pictures, I saw myself at 14, at 15, at 16. I felt the weight of that man's body, the pain, the disgust.

I am angered now and horrified. You see so clearly that I was used as if I was a disposable image. I am also angered and horrified to find that such limited exposure to pornography called up the memories and the behaviour patterns of my victimization so profoundly. I don't need studies and statistics to tell me that there is a relationship between pornography and real violence against women. My body remembers.

Mr. G: gay men and pornographic bookshops

MR. G: My name is --. I live at [address deleted]. I will speak under the ordinance of discussion as an individual not representing any organization. I am not a lawyer but I have been bothered by discussions of pornography as a First Amendment issue. The move to change the base of the Civil Rights area strikes me as an important tactic. My remarks aren't legalistic, they are general issues.

I am a gay man. I want to talk mainly to my gay brothers. We can easily find ourselves in ambivalent positions in where the distribution of pornography is.

For some gay communities, adult bookstores are main outlets for pornography material. They are — in fact, they serve as a meeting place and as a place to be sexual together. In a society of loving someone and being sexual with someone of the same sex, this can have severe negative consequences.

Gay men have to develop signals in order to recognize each other and cultivate places where we can feel relatively safe. Adult bookstores have come to be part of that picture. So I do not take lightly that such places will be lost to the gay community when the stores of pornography, this porn ordinance of pornography comes to be successful.

I would ask gay men to accept the teachership of women, to listen carefully to the points raised by women during these hearings. I have tried to do that here and on other contacts, and my personal conclusion is that gay men should accept the inconvenience of the world without adult bookshops in order to promote the survival of women, which is very much threatened by any situation that promotes pornography. And that is my main point.

I want to add something, looking toward the long range. Ordinances like this are important, but in my judgement pornography will only truly disappear from a society when all people are able to express their sexuality free and openly, or when the space now occupied by pornography is empty or perhaps better than that, be filled with eroticization of positive values by justice and respect. We are so far from that now that it is almost impossible to even imagine what this might be like.

I do have flashes of this vision now and again. I suspect all of you have such moments as well. My intuition tells me that gay men and progressive women are allies in elaborating this vision. I don't mean to exclude anyone but both of these groups are defined by outside values. Frequently these visions come from outsiders.

So my hope is that we can work together in the short term and in the long term rather than end up in whatever positions, divided positions. That is my hope. We are a long way from realizing that. I am committed to realizing that hope, it has shown kinds of thoughts that let me come here to ask our Council members to vote in favor of the ordinance. Thank you.

Ms. L, prostitutes' group PRIDE

CHAIRMAN WHITE: Ms. L.

MS L: I am -- [spelling out of name deleted]. I am the Outreach Advocate for a group called PRIDE. PRIDE is a self-help group for women who are or have been involved in the behaviour of prostitution. PRIDE is sponsored by the Minneapolis Family and Children's Services. As the Outreach Advocate, I would like to support the amending of the Civil Rights ordinance, and turn your attention to Section 5 — Number 2 specifically.

I was involved in the behaviour of prostitution for a period of three years. Since then, I have been involved with the PRIDE group for a year and a half. In my own experience and in working with women, I have become aware of the prevailing attitude that women who have been involved with prostitution are somewhat exempt from coercion. Therefore, I would like to emphasize the importance of the inclusion of Section 5, Number 2, letters aa through mm, as a part of this ordinance.

The same societal attitudes which support pornography also support prostitution. By allowing pornography to continue, our society is condoning and supporting the degradation of all women. Thank you.

CHAIRMAN WHITE: The next speaker.

Naomi Scheman: the need to listen

MS. SCHEMAN: My name is Naomi Scheman, S-c-h-e-m-a-n. I live in Ward 6. I am an Associate Professor of Philosophy and Director of Undergraduate Studies in Women's Studies at the University of

Minnesota.

I teach "Feminist Criticism of Concepts of the Self," I have taught it two or three times a year, this is my fifth year.

It is very clear to me in teaching that course what the connection is between pornography and freedom of speech, because over and over again in that class I have the students in the class discuss with me the experience that we all had here this evening. That is, women finding their voices, finding the ability to speak, often for the first time, and identifying what is in their lives, what the forces are in the society that have kept them silent for so long, that have forcibly kept them silent, that have chased any possible words out of their heads, that have given no ground to stand on and no voice to speak with. They speak within that class and within that class we learn how to speak the truth to each other, we learn how to hear it, learn how to articulate it, learn how to be clear about it.

The question is: What do we do when we go out of that class, what do we do when we go out of that class into that world that tells us that we are imagining it, we are making it up, that they are not like that? That these things do not happen to us or if they did there is nothing so terribly wrong? That is, we go back to the world that is structured by pornography and we lose our voices.

I believed every time I taught the class there is a problem with what to say to those women, what to suggest. With the anger they feel they often turn into a depression, they often retreat back into silence, they express the anger to those who are closest to them, sometimes they deserve it and sometimes they don't. But there has been as of yet no way of moving into the public world, moving into the society, moving into the world as structured and defined by the law, which matters because in our society's terms it tells us what is most real, what is most taken seriously, what most matters. There has been no way of moving back into that world and speaking the truth and expecting to be heard of, having that anger, of carrying one's voice outside the classroom, outside of small groups and friends into the world and having it taken seriously.

It has been different teaching that class this quarter. I have been able to say, "They are listening." There is an ordinance here, there is something that could become part of the law of the City in which we live that will enable us to speak the truth, that will enable us to be empowered. That will not empower the City of Minneapolis, that will not empower the police of Minneapolis, that will empower women to speak the truth and know that there is a space in this society, not just in isolated classrooms or friendship groups or support groups for that truth to be heard, taken seriously, believed and acted on. And it has been a different experience in teaching that course. I have been able to say to them, "It is not your own private anger any more, it is being listened to, taken seriously."

I am going to teach that course again in the summer. I don't want to have to go into that class saying "Well, they listened for a while. When it came to having the courage to provide the space for women, to listen, when it finally came to that they didn't come through and there still is no room in this society for your voice to be heard." I don't want to have to do

90

that.

Carrie Rickard, Women's Health Care Associates

CHAIRMAN WHITE: Carrie Rickard?

MS. RICKARD: My name is R-i-c-k-a-r-d. I am on the staff of Women's Health Care Associates, a private clinic in South Minneapolis. Our services include those of an obstetrics gynaecologist, certified nurse, midwives and nurse practitioner. Many of the women that come to our clinic have been sexually abused.

Dr. Patsy Parker, obstetrician and gynaecologist in our office, estimates that over 50 percent, over 100 of the women that she sees have told her of past or continuing sexual abuse. The emotional pain caused by the sexual abuse of these and of all women makes any promotion of that abuse intolerable, and a violation in and of itself. Pornography and these illegality of pornography suggests that the violent subjectification for women is okay. For that reason everybody at Women's Health Care Associates supports this Chair's amendment to ratify this ordinance.

CHAIRMAN WHITE: It is now that hour, those that added their names later on this evening if you would possibly come back we will begin at 5:00 o'clock tomorrow evening and hopefully you will be — well, you will be the first ones on the agenda to speak. So with that —

UNIDENTIFIED SPEAKER: Are you going to vote on Friday?

CHAIRMAN WHITE: I beg your pardon?

UNIDENTIFIED SPEAKER: The City Council?

CHAIRMAN WHITE: The City Council will, after the committee meeting tomorrow, we will vote whether to send it on to the City Council or not.

UNIDENTIFIED SPEAKER: But will they vote on Friday if you vote to send it on?

CHAIRMAN WHITE: If we move it out of committee it will be before the Council on Friday.

UNIDENTIFIED SPEAKER: What time would it be?

MS. HOYT: Mr. Chairman?

CHAIRMAN WHITE: Alderman Hoyt?

MS. HOYT: It was given its first reading and referred, it then has the public hearing. The Committee then takes an action and that action is either to vote it forward at the meeting or postpone it and go at a later meeting to collect more data or to send it forward with a recommendation for denial. That action is then forwarded to the Minneapolis City Council, they can agree with what the committee has said, they can reverse what the committee has said or they can hold it on the Council floor in search of further action.

Once they take an action on to the Minneapolis City Council it is then referred to the Mayor of the City of Minneapolis who has five working days in which to make a decision of whether to sign it, let it pass without signature, or to veto it. If it is vetoed, it comes back to the Minneapolis City Council for a decision of whether or not to override.

Be aware that in the City of Minneapolis all public speaking and testimony is done in committee in the Minneapolis City Council meeting. The only people who speak are the Council members themselves.

CHAIRMAN WHITE: Very well done, Councilmember Hoyt.

I think that what I am hearing, I am glad to spell it out, what I am hearing is there will be a vote on Friday and that what —

UNIDENTIFIED SPEAKER: And what time will it be?

CHAIRMAN WHITE: Well —

UNIDENTIFIED SPEAKER: We would like to be here.

CHAIRMAN WHITE: You understand that she said you can't speak but you can participate, you can sit.

UNIDENTIFIED SPEAKER: Right. So we want to know what time.

CHAIRMAN WHITE: Council starts at 9:30.

UNIDENTIFIED SPEAKER: 9:30 a.m.?

MS. HOYT: Council starts at 9:30 a.m. generally with 200 items on the agenda. It depends how much debating we have to do.

CHAIRMAN WHITE: Now, this can go forward to postpone until a further Council meeting before the end of the year, until then, because we do have a problem seriously with the Civil Rights Commission not being notified of their part in it. So we may have to pass it out of committee, dependent upon the Civil Rights, having the meeting with them and having the information before Friday.

MS. HOYT: Adjourned until 5:00 o'clock tomorrow?

CHAIRMAN WHITE: Adjourned until 5:00 o'clock tomorrow.

(Hearing adjourned until 5:00 o'clock in the afternoon of Tuesday, December 13, 1983.)

SESSION III

CHAIRMAN WHITE: The subcommittee of the Government Operations of Health and Social Services will come to order. There is a Ways and Means meeting in the other room across the hall that has two of our members, of our committee. And when they get through they will come over here. But the Ways and Means and Budget is a very important aspect of the City government.

Valerie Harper: pornography and show business

I would like to begin this meeting with an honor that I was a receipient of. Valerie Harper, those of you know her as Rhoda, she gave me a long distance call and I talked with her for about 20 minutes. And she told me she had sent a letter in strong support and she is going to get other support from other actresses and other people who live in Hollywood, to send telegrams and mail to me as Chairman of the Government Operations. And the letter I have before me: since Professor MacKinnon has amazed me ever since I heard her in Zoning and Planning, I would like you to read this letter from Valerie Harper.

MS. MacKINNON: Well, I was inspired by Andrea Dworkin when I was in the Zoning Committee, I was inspired by Andrea Dworkin so would you like to read it?

"To the City Council of the City of Minneapolis: It is a pleasure and a privilege to participate in this hearing, even if only by letter. I want to acknowledge the City Council and everyone involved in these discussions for collectively taking such an historic and beneficial step.

"The damage that pornography has done and continues to do to every woman, child, and man in our society is of such enormous proportion as to be practically immeasurable. The pornographic, and untrue image of human beings abounds. Because we are living within such an image, it is sometimes difficult to see and painful to confront. But we must, as you are in these hearings. Extensive research inalterably proves the connection, both direct and indirect, of pornography to violence, assaults and crimes against women (and children and men as well). I am therefore thankful for the opportunity to share my personal experience of pornography with this assembly.

"Approximately six years ago on an evening when I was about to film a segment of 'Rhoda', the CBS series in which I played the title role, I was presented with a gift by three co-workers. I opened the package to find a framed likeness of myself that measured about eight inches by ten inches. It was not a photograph but rather a sketch and the face was absolutely recognizable as me. It was a full length figure, naked except for high heeled shoes and stockings, taking off a shirt. Never in my life had I posed for any photograph, drawing, or painting remotely similar to this image. The people giving me this laughed, thought it was funny, thought I would find it funny, and truly meant no harm — they are all talented, intelligent, nice people, an indication of the extent of the pornographic mind set we all suffer under. I felt upset, ripped-off, diminished, insulted, abused, hurt, furious and powerless. All of which I concealed from my friends by smiling and saying 'Where did you get this?' (For the moment I thought they had had it made up by the art department at the studio.) 'From a magazine,' was the answer. Added to the aforementioned reactions was horror! I thought, 'This has been published! It is publicly available for anyone to see and assume I may have posed for it.'

"I curtailed my honest reaction because in a few minutes we would all have to begin filming our show — which we did. They thinking it had been a fun joke, me in a great deal of pain and distress.

"Subsequently I saw the same drawing in a magazine, I believe was called *Chic*. In one corner was a short rhyme or limerick alluding to Rhoda although not using the name Valerie Harper. However, a short time later, I was told about an advertisement in *Hustler* magazine which I saw. It was for T-shirts called Shock Tops that people could send away for. The buyer had their choice of seven famous women pictured in the nude; all of our full names were listed and, of course, choice of color of T-shirt. I was appalled and angry and had meetings with a laywer regarding what action I should take. All my then advisors, this attorney, my personal manager (regarding career) and my business manager (regarding accounting and finances) advised strongly against taking any action whatsoever. They all concurred that it would be extremely costly and would draw attention to and sell more of these shirts.

"I retained another laywer who in several phone calls seemed to scare the magazine sufficiently as to discontinue the advertisement. We checked the magazine the following issue and the ad was not there. From there I dropped the whole matter, hoping it was over but feeling quite incomplete and unsatisfied about it.

"As a young dancer-actress-singer in New York City, I experienced firsthand (and have heard countless accounts from many other women in these fields and modeling) continual attemps to convince that pornography, photography, films, et cetera were a stepping stone to stardom. Young people and children are particularly vulnerable to this

94

kind of enticement in New York City and Los Angeles as they are show business centers. A common statement was, and may still be 'Marilyn Monroe did that calendar and look what she became.'

"Also, during the audition process, actresses, singers, dancers, models are extremely vulnerable. I know of instances when women have entered the audition room to find the man who would be giving the job, completely nude. Point blank proposals of sexual service as part of getting the job are extremely common.

"A real fear now exists in terms of the horror of snuff movies, films in which women's actual murders have been recorded and then presented as pornographic entertainment. The audition process in unscrupulous hands can put the job applicant at tremendous risk.

"A detective in NYC, New York City, cited a case to me of a pornography ring in Manhattan that enticed young models to an office supposedly for a job interview. Once there the young women were attacked, subdued by beating or drugs and then photographed in hideous pornographic poses, tied, tortured, bound to trees in sexual union with animals, several men and on and on. When they came to or were released, it was with the warning that if they contacted the police all the polaroid shots of them would be sent to their parents, places of business, schools and so forth."

"The police officer told me it wasn't until scores of women were so victimized in this manner that one finally took it to the authorities. This group had been doing millions of dollars worth of business.

"I have been working with the Rape Treatment Center of Santa Monica Hospital for almost five years now (adacent to LA area). It is the opinion of the staff there that rape, sexual and physical assaults on women and children are definitely linked to pornography as a particular climate is created by its use, acceptability, and encouragement. More and more brutal and sadistically violent attacks are occurring with alarming frequency, as are attacks and sexual assaults on children (often within their own families).

"It would be a massive move in the right direction to create in the law a recourse for victims and future victims, a deterrent to current and would be pornographers and a new context within which human beings could live their lives. A context of support, sharing, love and contribution to one another. True partnership on our planet. Thank you — Valerie Harper."

MS. DWORKIN: Mr. Chirman, may I put into evidence, I won't read it, it is a letter: To whom it may concern by Jamie Lee Bauer who talks about her own exploitation by pornography.

CHAIRMAN WHITE: Yes, just put it into the record.

But I am also aware that Valerie Harper sent you the T-shirt but we won't show that.

Now, to reiterate my discretion, I would like to limit the speakers to three minutes.

I am going to allow Bill Neiman of the Hennepin County Attorney's Office to speak because of his having to get out of here for some reason he didn't explain to me. But I am certain that it is important.

Bill Neiman, would you come and speak briefly?

Bill Neiman: presence of pornography at scene of crime

MR. NEIMAN: Thank you. Bill Neiman, Assistant County Attorney in the Hennepin County Attorney's Office. And I appreciate being taken out of order. The reason is I have to get back home to take care of my children.

CHAIRMAN WHITE: Okay, I didn't know that.

MR. NEIMAN: The reason I was asked by Councilmember Hoyt to speak today regarding the subject is because I have been in the Hennepin County Attorney's Office for five years and on the team of attorneys who prosecute all sexual assault cases and child abuse cases at Hennepin County.

In brief, the background: our office did support and did draft the bill which was passed a year ago that makes virtually all forms of child pornography a felony. Now in terms of the relationship between pornography and sexual assault and child abuse, what I am best equipped to talk to you about is what I have seen as prosecutor, having reviewed hundreds, certainly a hundred or more cases involving sexual assault of adults or the sexual abuse of children.

Now I should emphasize, and this is important to understand, that generally speaking with pornography, materials are seized or found at the time of the arrest or shortly after the arrest. It is not with a purpose, that is the police are not looking for those materials so that when I talk about the numbers I am about to speak of, I say that with the understanding that I have little doubt that if the police in each case where they suspected sexual assault looked for material of this type, if they did they would find a much greater number than are found. I say that because quite a number are found without any special effort being made to look for pornographic materials.

Now in cases involving adults, primarily women, that is women, female victims, pornographic materials are often found. I would not say in a majority of cases but a substantial percent of cases, those materials are found in or near where the person lives, or say the motor vehicle which was used to transport the assailant to the place of the sexual assault.

We do see with children a much greater use of pornographic materials. I would say that in the cases that I had, that I have had, and I have had many of them, that pornographic materials are found, if not in the majority of cases, very close to he majority of cases found in the home of the person who is sexually abusing the chidren and often there are very substantial numbers of pornographic materials. These pornographic materials are both adult and children.

Now, an example, and I could give you many examples, an example of a recent case I had or I have, actually where such materials were being used, just for the Committee's information, this young girl was raped I believe by her stepfather, a live-in boy friend. And one of the things that he did as part of the sexual assault of the girl is he would sit on the toilet undressed and she would be undressed in the bathroom and he would have her, while undressed, hold up for example the centerfold of a magazine that depicted a naked woman or whatever. And while she was holding this and standing naked herself, he would masturbate himself. And this use is not extraordinary, it is no more bizarre or less bizzare a use of pornographic material that we have seen. So I think it is fair to say from the point of view of the Hennepin County Attorney's Office that we have found pornography to be used very substantially where children are the victims and substantially where adults are the victims. Thank you.

MS. DWORKING: May I ask you one question?

CHAIRMAN WHITE: I wanted to ask one too.

MS. DWORKING: I am sorry, please?

CHAIRMAN WHITE: Under Section 1 139.10 in the ending sentence of that paragraph it reads, "Such discriminatory practices degrade individuals, foster intolerance and hate, and create and intensify unemployment, substandard housing, under-education, ill health, lawlessness and poverty, thereby injuring the public welfare." As an attorney dealing with all of those things, what does that sentence say to you?

MR. NEIMAN: In terms of pornography, well, my personal belief is that pornography does cause people to act out criminally, sexually, criminally in a sexual fashion, sometimes in a physical aggressive fashion. My personal belief is that there is a relationship. I don't have scientific evidence of that but I have simply seen too many cases to believe otherwise. That is how I would read that sentence and it is hard — as stated, it is hard to describe something which has that terrible impact as anything other than discriminatory when the impact it has on the victims is as great as it is.

CHAIRMAN WHITE: Thank you.

MS.MacKINNON: Would you say it is against the public welfare?

MR. NEIMAN: I would say that given what happens to the victims in these cases, especially the child victims that are often, if not destroyed, partially ruined for life, that if it had that effect on one victim it would have a terrible effect — I think it has that effect on hundreds of children.

MS. MacKINNON: Have you found the taking of pictures to be part of these things you see?

MR. NEIMAN: We have seen —

MS. MacKINNON: In the course of your work?

MR. NEIMAN: Yes, I have. And others in the office have prosecuted these cases. Frankly, I think there is much more of it than we have had the good fortune to discover. And in fact, our office is presently trying to develop a somewhat more sophisticated approach to locating, arresting, and prosecuting pornographers. The persons that we have found we have prosecuted, and I believe they have been involved sexually with the children, my personal belief is that although we have had some success, there is much more out there that we haven't been able to locate or find as a sophisticated offense and it is difficult to get to the perpetrator. Thank you.

CHAIRMAN WHITE: Thank you very much.

The next speaker, and please, we would like to get out of here, I know how you feel but we don't have the time that I would like to have here this evening. so if you would hold your statements to four minutes, as closely as possible to it, I would appreciate it.

The next speaker would be Wanda Richardson.

MS. MacKINNON: Ms. G, I believe would be first if she is here and then -- -- and then -- --.

MS. M: pornography as blueprint for assault

MS. M: Before I begin, I have to say that I am unable to state what my relationship is to the people I am going to talk about because many of them are still victims whose lives are in danger.

For the majority of my life, I lived with a divorced woman and her children in the house that she owned. Her ex-husband also lived in the house we lived in. He would not leave. He threatened to kill the woman if she ever tried to get help in getting him away from her and out of her house.

Over a period of 18 years the woman was regularly raped by this man. He would bring pornographic magazines, books, and paraphernalia into the bedroom with him and tell her that if she did not perform the sexual acts that were being done in the "dirty" books and magazines he would beat her and kill her. I know about this because my bedroom was right next to hers. I could hear everything they said. I could hear her screams and cries. In addition, since I did most of the cleaning in the house, I would often come across the books, magazines, and paraphernalia that were in the bedroom and other rooms of the house. The magazines had pictures of mostly women and children and some men. Eventually, the woman admitted to me that her ex-husband did in fact use pornography materials to terrorize and rape her.

Not only did I suffer through the torture of listening to the rapes and tortures of a woman, but I could see what grotesque acts this man was performing on her from the pictures in the pornographic materials. I was also able to see the systematic destruction of a human being taking place before my eyes.

At the time I lived with the woman, I was completely helpless, powerless in regard to helping this woman and her children in getting away from this man. I was told by the man that if I ever told anyone about the things that he did or if I ever tried to run away, that he would beat me, that he would break and cut off my arms and legs, that he would cut up my face so that no man would ever want to look at me, that he would kill me, and that he would make me sorry that I ever told on him.

During the time that I was held captive by that man, I was physically and psychologically abused by him, I was whipped with belts and electrical cords. I was beat with pieces of wood. I was usually forced to pull my pants down before I was to be beaten. I was touched and grabbed where I did not want him to touch me. I was also locked into dark closets and the

98

basement for many hours at a time and I was often not allowed to speak or cry.

The things that this man did to me were also done to the children of the woman, except that they suffered from even worse abuse. I believe that part of the psychological abuse I suffered from was from the pornographic materials that the man used in his terrorization of us. I knew that if he wanted to, he could do more of these things that were being done in those magazines to me. When he looked at the magazines, he could make hateful, obscene, violent remarks about women in general and about me. I was told that because I am female I am here to be used and abused by him and that because he is male he is the master and I am his slave.

I was terrorized into keeping silent and it wasn't until three years after escaping from him that I was psychologically and emotionally strong enough to tell anyone what had happened to me.

I am not saying that pornography caused that man to do those things to me and to other women and children. I am saying that pornography is an extension of the violence and hatred against women that already exists in this society. To get rid of pornography is to get rid of part of the violence against women that permeates this society.

Pornography makes a mockery of the torture, beatings, rapes, mutilations, degradations and killings that I and other women have suffered from, all for men's sexual gratification.

Every time I walk into a neighborhood grocery store or drug store I am reminded that if I don't watch my step, do what I'm told, keep silent or stay in my place, that I could end up like one of the women in that pornographic material being sold in those stores.

I believe what those magazines say because it has happened to me.

The last statement that I have to make is a political one. If someone wants to study the condition of women in this society, all that person has to do is to view a pornographic book, magazine, or movie. Pornography is an example of a picture of a diagram with instructions of how to degrade a woman. It is a blueprint of the state of women's conditions in the society. Pornography tells the truth about women's conditions. But pornography lies about how we think and feel about our condition.

MS. MacKINNON: Chairman White, a woman named Angelia Wright got in touch with me this morning and I would like to submit her written statement. Perhaps it would be better if I didn't read it and put it in. It is a statement with detail and just like the statement that was just made.

CHAIRMAN WHITE: As I said last night, it takes quite a bit to sit and stand, as last night, before all the eyes and ears that are looking and let forth and let it all hang out and tell what happened to someone. It is something I will never forget.

Ms. U, please?

Ms. U: Pornography, racism and rape

MS. U: First I want to thank my friends for coming to support me today. It's scary to stand before you and talk of something so painful. It

99

helps me having women on the Council, it makes it a little easier. I wish more of you were people of color.

I would like to direct my story, even though he is not here, to Mark Kaplan because I am from his ward. He represents many women of color and by his vote on this ordinance he can give us a safer community in which to live.

When I was first asked to testify I resisted some because the memories are so painful and so recent. I am here because of my four-year-old daughter and other Indian children. I want them to grow up in a more healthful and loving society.

I was attacked by two white men and from the beginning they let me know they hated my people, even though it was obvious from their remarks they knew very little about us. And they let me know that the rape of a "squaw" by white men was practically honored by white society. In fact, it has been made into a video game called *Custer's Last Stand*. And that's what they screamed in my face as they threw me to the ground, "This is more fun than *Custer's Last Stand*."

They held me down and as one was running the tip of his knife across my face and throat he said, "Do you want to play *Custer's Last Stand*? It's great. You lose but you don't care, do you? You like a little pain, don't you squaw?" They both laughed and then he said, "There is a lot of cock in *Custer's Last Stand*. You should be grateful, squaw, the All-American boys like us want you. Maybe we will tie you to a tree and start a fire around you."

They made other comments, "The only good Indian is a dead Indian." "A squaw out alone deserves to be raped." Words that still terrorize me today.

It may surprise you to hear stories that connect pornography and white men raping women of color. It doesn't surprise me. I think pornography, racism, and rape are perfect partners. They all rely on hate. They all reduce a living person to an object. A society that sells books, movies, and video games like *Custer's Last Stand* on its street corners gives white men permission to do what they did to me. Like they said, I'm scum. It is a game to track me down, rape and torture me.

So I bring my screams of that night here to you today, hoping that they will help you decide to stand against the dehumanization and violence of pornography. I would like to end with a poem that I wrote about my nightmares after my attack.

"I used to welcome the first shadows of night as they slid along the edge of day. The thunderbird closing her eyes slowly, softly pulling us all into the beauty of the darkness and the dream.

"Now the shadows hide danger and hatred. The thunderbird screams her warning of the terror of the darkness and the nightmare.

"The hoop of the universe is broken. Sacred eagle feathers are strewn on the ground where they throw me, naked, to play out *Custer's Last Stand*.

"Knives slash red streaks. Mean, twisted faces, large rough hands, swirl and chase me through the darkness. I struggle awake just as the owl calls my name."

MS. DWORKIN: Mr Chairman, just for the record I just want to say that the actual name of the video game which portrays the rape that was described here and that was actually lived through is *Custer's Revenge.*

CHAIRMAN WHITE : Ms. C, are you here?

MS. MacKINNON: Chairman, she is coming in a car, she is trying to get a ride. She may be a little bit late, we should just proceed.

CHAIRMAN WHITE: Then Wanda Richardson.

Wanda Richardson: Pornography and battering

MS. RICHARDSON: I work at Harriet Tubman Women's Shelter. I was asked to speak about the connection that we see at the shelter between pornography and violence against women. What I would like to say is not only my own thoughts and experience, it is also that of many other women both working at the shelter and women who have come to the shelter.

The first thing that I would like to say is that there is a very similar status between women who are battered and women in pornography. Battered women are reduced to being physical objects. They are no longer people, they have no rights, they have no dignity. They are just objects and things. Women in pornography are also reduced to the level of objects and things. They don't exist as human beings but they are merely there to satisfy a man's desire.

In the case of battering, we see women existing as something men have there to vent their feelings on. In pornography they are there supposedly for sexual desire. Pornography is a classic example of the objectification of women. We see results of that every day at our shelter.

I would say that in many cases a lot of violence that we see really has nothing to do with sex or anger or anything else. It really is just a power relationship, where there is a great deal of inequality between men and women and men are just using that to their advantage to carry those things out. There is a lot of sex and violence, both in battering situations and in pornography. If you look at a lot of pornography it shows women being beaten, humiliated, tied up. It shows women tied and stabbed, poked, prodded and abused by devices, assaulted by several men or animals and many ugly and degrading things. When you see a woman being battered, you see a lot of the same ugliness and violence at the same time. Not only do they portray women as liking and deserving this sexual abuse, it shows them as enjoying it, deserving it, and that is what one of the great myths of battery is, is that women deserve to be battered and that they enjoy it. If they didn't like it they wouldn't stay.

Men look at women in pornography magazines; they say the same things about them. They like it, they enjoy it. The women coming to the shelter say over and over again the men say that to them, "You enjoy this, you deserve it." Men look at pornography and they observe that message, the women liking and deserving that treatment. They act it out on specific women, usually their girl friends and wives, sometimes anonymous, like rape on the street. What they are doing are acting out the messages that women are not human beings, they are objects.

There is many specific cases that I could cite, I don't want to go into it now. I would like to say we have many, many examples of women coming to the shelter who have cases of combined sexual and physical assault where the violence and the sex is intertwined but you can't tell the difference, closely intertwined. They are a target not only for violence but also seen as sexually appealing. And a lot of times this is acted out at home where men will beat a woman and find that very sexually arousing. Many of the women come and say that immediately after battering or shortly thereafter the man wants sex and they said, "How could he want men after he has done this to me, how could he expect me, how could he expect me not to be upset like nothing has happened, and to them nothing has happened." To the woman it has been a degrading experience and to the man it has been sexually exciting.

If you look at any pornographic magazine you will see the answer to those questions that the women are asking. We had two recent cases that I would like to cite, one in which a woman was taken repeatedly by her boy friend to the Rialto Theater and made to watch X rated movies. And then he would take her home and force her to act out with him these movies. Of course, a lot of these movies contain extreme violence. After one of these episodes she ended up in hospital, that is how she came to our shelter.

In another case a woman was imprisoned in the house by her husband. He had a video cassette recorder and he would bring home pornographic movies and tie her to a chair and force her to act out what they were seeing on the screen. Of course, she was eventually severely injured and again came to our shelter.

These are just two examples. They are not by any means unusual ones. These things happen all the time.

The effects on the women of this kind of abuse, of course, there is the physical abuse which we see and deal with every day. But there is a tremendous amount of emotional abuse, mental abuse, that is they are degraded and humiliated by the pornography and the violence. There is a tremendous loss of self-esteem and self-worth. A lot of times that is what they feel like, that is all they are worth. They are only bodies and they don't deserve anything better than that treatment. They have no rights or respect, either from others or from themselves.

I would also like to point out that a lot of this information that we have gotten from women of the shelter has not been looked for. We don't have specific questions on our intakes about sexual abuse and violence. Most of this comes out during the discussion that we have when the woman first comes. And as we have seen it over and over again, the women saying the same things, where you have many separate incidents itself but a lot of similar occurrences. You start seeing a pattern and you start saying, "Where is this pattern coming from?"

Well, it is coming from socialization from cultural images. And the strongest influence that we have been able to find on this type of treatment of women is pornography. Many of the women said that pornography is around their house. They say, "He has been to the theaters, he does this and he does that and he sees these things. He comes home and he acts it out on me or he makes me act it out also." We think that pornography is probably the most extreme example of antiwomen socialization that men receive in this society. We don't believe that men are born to be sexually and physically abusive to women, they learn this. And the main place they learn this is through pornography. We see the victims of this every day.

I would like to finish up by saying that because we have seen so much of this and it does seem to be increasing, that we are going to be adding questions on our intake to try and document the connection between pornography and violence. We are going to try to be collecting some data, hopefully that will be helpful for proceedings such as this. Thank you.

CHAIRMAN WHITE: Thank you. I can understand, but please try to hold it to four minutes. We have got so many people, four minutes, please.

Sharon Rice Vaughn and Donna Dunn: testimony of battery victims

MS. RICE VAUGHN: My name is Sharon Rice Vaughn and I work at the Minnesota Coalition for Battered Women which is in St. Paul. I would like to read testimony from Donna Dunn from Rochester, have you called her name? She says that the storm started there this morning and that she was all dressed in her dress with her testimony and couldn't get here because of the snow. Would that be all right? I would like to start with that and finish with mine.

CHAIRMAN WHITE: Okay. Do this as expeditiously as you can.

MS. RICE VAUGHN: Yes, I will. And I will identify Donna Dunn.

Donna Dunn works at Women's Shelter, Incorporated in Rochester, Minnesota. She is also a member of the Board of Directors of the Minnesota Coalition for Battered Women.

This is Donna's statment: "I am taking part in today's testimony regarding pornography in order to bring you some information about how pornography has contributed to the abuse of some women we have come in contact with at Women's Shelter in Rochester. Women's Shelter is a home for battered women and their children. Women's Shelter has operated as a shelter for five years. In that time over 800 women have stayed with us. An additional 500 women contact the shelter each year in need of assistance, advocacy, and/or support.

"Our experience in working with battered women has led us to a clear understanding of the way our society supports, allows and even encourages male violence against women. The incapacity to identify women as valuable contributing members of American society, the continuing consistence in identifying and validating women in terms of their relationships or service to men, contributes to the extreme isolation of all women, particularly battered women.

"In experience, we are finally beginning to create an atmosphere in

103

which battered women can identify, talk about, and seek help, support in escaping abuse and violence. While broken bones, concussions, broken teeth, ripped out hair and beatings that render women unconscious are now frequently shared stories from battered women, sexual assault within sexual relationships remains all too frequently behind the veil of privacy, a sense of privacy that is a result of a society in which a woman learns from birth that her body is not her own and that her sense of worth is defined by those who would use her body.

"Historically, women have been denied their own sexuality and along with that the right to make decisions about how they are used sexually. This lack of decision making power combined with society's victimization of the woman who is sexually assaulted creates a sense of shame, of guilt, of dirtiness that disallows her to speak of the sexual assault even within the safe atmosphere of the shelter.

"Particulars about the use of pornography and its perpetuation of abuse are not a part of our regular data collection. However, we at Women's Shelter, Inc. know it to be a fact that pornography contributes to the battering of women and children.

"While doing our intake procedure and in the ongoing close contact with shelter advocates pornography is frequently stated as a hobby of the abuser. We would like to give you three examples of how pornography encourages the ongoing beatings and rape of women we know. Number one, one woman known to us related that her spouse always had a number of pornographic magazines around the house. The final episode that resulted in ending the marriage was his acting out a scene from one of the magazines. She was forcibly stripped, bound and gagged. And with the help from her husband, she was raped by a German Shepherd. His second wife became known to us when she sought support because of the magazines and bondage equipment she found in their home.

"Number two: another woman spoke of her husband's obsession with tying women up. She said he had rape and bondage magazines all over the house. She discovered two suitcases full of Barbie dolls with ropes tied on their arms and legs and tape across their mouths. She added, 'He used to tie me up and he tried those things on me.' But she also stated that she had not recognized this as sexual abuse. This statement from her reinforces our earlier contention that she did not have the freedom to identify sexual assault because she felt no ownership of her own body.

"Number three: *Penthouse* and *Hustler* were always a part of the literature in the third woman's home. Occasionally her spouse would add *Cheri, Oui, Swedish Erotica* to the collection. His favorite form of abuse was bondage. He enjoyed playing what he called a game of whipping and slavery. She knows that what he did to her was directly related to articles about bondage and sex lays which he read. He wanted to involve a second woman, her friend, in the scenarios. Her refusal to comply with his demands resulted in her being violently anally assaulted. She stated, 'Even if he had not gotten these specific ideas from the magazines, the magazines reinforced his attitude about women and his attitude that he could do what he wanted with me.'

104

"Our experience at Women's Shelter indicates and even demands that we as a society recognize and be accountable for the very specific ways in which individual women are hurt and the role that pornography plays in that hurt. It is because of that connection that I submit this testimony to you."

I would like to say, from working in two shelters and working with the Coalition for a total of 11 years that Wanda said for all of us, I think, a lot of things that I won't repeat. But I think I can add to them.

One thing that battered women and women of — victims of pornography have in common is an irony. Battered women and women that are victims of pornography are invisible in this culture. This ordinance is the beginning of defining their visibility and it is extremely important that it pass, and it does not go nearly far enough.

Battered women, until about 10 years ago, were invisible. They were told to turn the other cheek. They went through the revolving door of emergency rooms. Nobody wanted to help them and that is the classic way of creating a victimless crime. You don't have a victim, she is so invisible she doesn't exist.

When a woman is blamed for the assault that is done to her, she does not exist. She is invisible in this society. That is something that has begun to change, it hasn't changed nearly enough. Women do have options.

If a woman is invisible as a victim of a crime, she has nowhere to go. She literally has no options. This ordinance is the beginning of options, and it is small.

Another thing that women have in common, those who are battered and victims of pornography, they are part of an epidemic that is an irony of their visibility. They are not victims of social psychopathic deviants, there is an epidemic of women against battering of women. Battery happens in the home, it is private, battering is sanctified pornography. Battering happens behind the lace curtain of the sacred home and it is a form of pornography and an act of pornography.

There are 40,000 women in Minnesota who are estimated by the Department of Corrections to be 40,000 incidents of battering of women per year, which is an underestimation. And 10 years ago there were none. It wasn't even a category of crime.

The FBI has called battering the nation's most under-reported crime. It estimates, which is an underestimate, that a woman is beaten every 18 seconds. What we know about the epidemic of pornography is that it is a seven billion dollar industry in this country. The entire National, Federal, AFDC budget is eight billion dollars. Pornography is one billion below that. Both involve women who are hurt in every way. They are hurt psychologically, they are hurt physically, and they are hurt sexually. And the combination of what it does to a woman is that, as women have said who talk to shelter residents, that they don't even define it as rape.

If you ask a woman has she been raped, in an intake, she says no. If you ask her if sex is forced on her, she says yeah, of course it has. I mean, that is where we are. We don't even have a definition of what has happened to women.

I would like to urge you to pass the ordinance and I thank you for holding this testimony. You realize what you have done, you have opened this flood gate of women who have been here to listen to them. And every woman has a story to tell.

CHAIRMAN WHITE: You most certainly are correct. The flood gates are open, you should see my desk.

Barbara Chester?

Barbara Chester: permission to rape

MS. CHESTER: I am here to speak for some of those women that have stories and can't be here to tell them.

Presently I am the Director of the Rape and Sexual Assault Center in Hennepin County. Pornography, like rape, is not about sex but about control, hostility and violence. I have read in some of our papers that there has been suggested that there is no connection between pornography and sexual violence because there has never been a case on record of a man walking into an adult bookstore and exiting 10 minutes later to pounce on a victim. I would agree and add that since our first big study on rape back in 1971, we know that rape is a planned act, rape is not an act of impulse. It is an act that is well nurtured in our society.

Rape is a social disease that is born in an environment that links sex with violence and humiliation. For two years I ran a group with another woman at one of the men's correctional facilities in Minnesota. All of these men, almost all these men, were violent offenders and had committed rape. Although only in 12 years, only one was in prison for rape. One man in our group admitted to raping over 100 women. I might say bragged about raping over 100 women. He also admitted masturbating to hard-core pornography before his crimes. Almost every one of the men in the group admitted to masturbating to fantasies of violence. And most of them acted out this violence against women or children.

Let us use our common sense for a moment. When two things are linked by something visual we associate the two. When this association is reinforced, it is likely to become a repeated behavior.

Some of them say it is a catharsis, if they look at pictures of women being slashed and humiliated, then they won't have to do this in real life, parents beating children and/or child abuse. Yet no one would suggest that we all look at films of parents beating children in order to end child abuse or to watch films of Blacks, Indians, and Hispanics being handcuffed and humiliated in order to end racism. There is no reason then to suspect that pictures of bound and mutilated women will decrease misogyny. Indeed, as many offenders in my experience have noted, masturbating to fantasies of these images is extremely reinforcing and in many cases led to their acts of sexual violence.

We have seen cases at our own and other rape centers in Minnesota, cases like one involving a mentally handicapped women being taken to an apartment, handcuffed to a steam pipe, having food shoved into her vagina while dogs licked it out to the amusement of the spectator. Cases

106

like the women who was tied by her heels and suspended upside down and forced to perform oral intercourse with her husband, who later raped her in the bathroom after urinating and defecating on her. Cases like the man who never had intercourse with his wife unless it was in front of other men he brought home from the local bar. I wonder where these ideas came from?

Many of us reacted with shock and horror to the gang rape of a woman on a pool table in a bar in New Bedford in March of 1983, while bystanders cheered and applauded. Yet in the January issue of *Hustler* a layout appeared of this exact scenario, a woman spread-eagled on a pool table being gang raped. I wonder if any of the participants in New Bedford two months later were readers of *Hustler*.

Permission to violate once given cannot be constrained. There is no such thing as "slightly violated" or "a little bit raped". Because sexual violence is a continuum, not a hierarchy. Pornography is the permission and direction and rehearsal for sexual violence. It is the rape of our fantasy lives and ultimately, the rape of our bodies.

MS. MacKINNON: I have a letter from Marvin Lewis to the City Council, who is bringing cases for women against psychotherapists who abuse their authority. I know we also have a statement by a woman who works with prostitutes, stating that many girls and young women are directed into pornography and making a movie by being threatened with physical harm. And the pictures are being taken and told they are for private use, and later are sold.

MS. DWORKIN: We also have a letter form Dr. Phyllis Chesler who is a psychotherapist who describes in detail the effects of pornography on women's self-esteem and who believes that pornography leads to chronic depression, self-hatred, and other extremely damaging psychological states.

And also a letter from Family and Children's Services here in Minneapolis, Minnesota. Specifically about pornographic abuse of women in psychotherapy by psychotherapists. The uses of women in pornography to exploit women.

CHAIRMAN WHITE: Let the record show these.

Okay, am I saying this correctly, the next speaker is Daryl Dahlheimer, I hope I am saying it correctly.

Daryl Dahlheimer: work with sex offenders.

MR. DAHLHEIMER: You are.

Well, I think I have a lot to say that is similar, I will try to skip over the parts that are repetitive.

I do wish to say, and I am not embarrassed to be repetitive, that we have been silent too long on the issue. I am pleased we are spending a lot of time on the particular issue. As you announced, my name is Daryl Dahlheimer and I am going to try to talk about the connection of sexual violence and some of the offenders I work with and pornography.

My background is a psychotherapist who has worked with both victims

107

and perpetrators of sexual violence. I spent the past two years working with male felons in an alternative-to-prison treatment program in Hennepin County, approximately half of whom are sex offenders. I can't claim to hold any definitive or rigorous scientific data on the subject.

I tried hard to answer the following questions in my practice. First, what changes are necessary in the offenders' values and beliefs in order to assure that he will not revictimize someone? And secondly, what factors contribute to sexually violent behavior? I would like to share some of my conclusions so far.

CHAIRMAN WHITE: Excuse me, could you lift that up a little more?

MR. DAHLHEIMER: Before I start I want to state several understandings so that we have common definitions. My understanding of sexual violence, with many forms, ranges from rape in marriage to sexual assault on the streets to incest in families. And the common ground of all of these is that sexual violence is prevalent in each of its forms, and is fundamentally assaultive, not sexual, with women being the primary target and women, excuse me, and men virtually having cornered the market on who is the aggressor.

The second understanding is that pornography is also prevalent, in both written and picture form, and is distinguishable from erotica or sex education material in that it specifically involves the demeaning or degrading representation of women, men, or children.

With that in mind, I'd like to tell you what I have learned in working with sex offenders. First, sexual violence is not the work of the insane or the inhuman. The rapist or molester is always seen as a stranger, working in alleys and school yards, not as one of our own. This I believe blurs the truth that sexual violence is learned behavior and that we are all capable of rape. Nicholas Groth, one of the leading researchers in the area, identified that 95 percent of the rapes fall into patterns of anger in which sexuality becomes a hostile act, or power in which sexuality becomes an expression of conquest. I want to stress hostility and conquest are the primary motivations in 95 percent of the rape studies.

Consider the following verbatim statement by several rapists who Groth interviewed: "I wanted to knock the woman off her pedestal, and I felt rape was the worst thing I could do to her, she wanted it, she was asking for it. She just said 'No' so I wouldn't think she was easy." I wish to state that we are witnessing violent acts but often women are pictured smiling, enjoying it. There are statements accompanying these pictures and articles to the extent that women are supposedly wishing to give in. So I wish to, you know, call your attention to the fact that in terms of their own motives, there is some connections between the pornography and what is going on with these offenders.

Secondly, sexual beliefs of men who are sexually violent tend to be the following: women are perceived as seductive, manipulating, powerful. Men are dichotomized into strong or weak, "studs" or "queers". He sees his task as one of conquering women and competing with men. a sexual encounter for him is getting something rather than sharing something. And I think if you take a look at the pretty graphic representations of what is mentioned, of what goes on in pornographic literature and images, I think you will see similar images between pornography and the basis of and outlooks of these offenders which brings me to my final point.

I want to help you understand some of the mechanisms by which pornography may end up reinforcing sexual violence or creating sexual violence.

First is the fact that the sex offenders, it is well documented, tend to view others, other people particularly women, more as objects or obstacles than as individuals. This is part of their belief system that separates these people from their humanity and treats them as objects. It is no secret that pornography can be objectification of women's bodies and women's sexualities. In that particular way it may be a reinforcement tool.

Second, we know in the psychotherapy field that imagination and visual imagery are powerful tools for shaping human behavior. It is no secret that violent images have led to increased violence in people and violent images and pornography may give them rationales, minimizing the pain, projection of blame, and other distortions along with the image.

The third is that we recognize as a society the importance of prohibiting hate-material toward minority groups. Given the fact that violent behavior has been shown to lead to imitative results after exposure to violence on TV, I think this mechanism may work for the offenders.

It feels crazy to many of us working in therapy with offenders and victims that society is so silent on what looks to us like a clear link between written and visual images of victimization and acts of victimization. In both my professional capacity and as a resident of Minneapolis, I am grateful to this committee for taking steps to end this silence. Thank you.

CHAIRMAN WHITE: Those of you who do have notes, if you do read from them, please leave them with the City Clerk.

MS. MacKINNON: Mr. Chairman, I would like to submit some additional documentation on the exact points that were made by Mr. Dahlheimer. One is from a book called *The Rapist File*. It is interviews with rapists as they discussed, as did Mr. Dahlheimer, the use that the rapists themselves report making of pornography.

And I would also like to submit an interview excerpt written in the form of a book about Ted Bundy, the mass murderer of women, the interviews with him. Sections from that book. He said, this is the interviewer, he states, "Victims, you indicated that they would be symbols and images. But I'm not really sure. Images of what?" And Ted exclaimed, "Of women. I mean, of the idealized woman. What else can I say?" The interviewer, "A stereotype?" This is Bundy, "No, they wouldn't be stereotypes necessarily. But they would be reasonable facsimilies to women as a class. A class not of women, per se, but a class that has almost been created through the mythology of women and how they are used as objects." This is the basis on which he chose which women to kill.

CHAIRMAN WHITE: Okay.

MS. MacKINNON: I would also like to submit a report from the — it's an ongoing criminal case from which I have removed the names. I do have

109

the names, I have the name of the one victim who is not a minor. I don't have the victims who are minors.

It describes a young woman who was abducted by a man who branded her and who burned her viciously. And a number of other monstrosities. The same man is being, is also simultaneously being tried for the abuse of several minors in which his modus operandi appears to be, from the allegations in the complaint, that he would pick up young girls, show them pornographic movies, keep them prisoners for several days, up to a week or whenever they could escape, during which time they were tortured, raped etcetera. So I am submitting those two complaints with all of their numbers on them but with the names of the individuals removed by me.

CHAIRMAN WHITE: Let the record show.

Is that the last one you read from, is this something within the State of Minnesota?

MS. DWORKING: Yes.

MS. MacKINNON: Yes, this last — the ones with the names deleted. I believe it is, Chairman White, it is the State of Minnesota and the papers do reflect. Everything is on the papers except the names of the individuals.

CHAIRMAN WHITE: Bill Seals.

Bill Seals: controlling sexual assault

MR. SEALS: Good evening, my name is Bill Seals. I am the Director of Sexual Assault Services at the Center for Behavior Therapy in Minneapolis. I have worked with hundreds of sex offenders over the past 10 years.

Unfortunately, the relationship between pornography and sexual assault gets mixed reviews in the literature. My experience has been that pornography is often used by sex offenders as a stimulus to their sexually acting out. The sexual insecurity of sex offenders is reinforced by porn. Quite often sex offenders will use porn because they think of it as being safe. They live vicariously through the pictures. Eventually, that is not satisfying enough and they end up acting out sexually.

I believe we would have sex offenders even if we didn't have porn. I also believe that we must make safeguards and take the measures which are necessary to minimize sexual assault. Knowing that I was going to appear here, I asked 37 sex offenders of various types of sexual assult how many of them had actually used pornography prior to their sexually acting out. And of the 37, 35 of them stated that they had at one time or another. Not all the time, at one time or another.

Whenever we read about another sexual assault case in the paper, we instinctively react with rage. We cry out for stronger prison terms. Seldom, however, do we ask why. Seldom do we look at the causes. Perhaps if we take a look at those causes, which include pornography, we might find that we have more control over preventing sexual assault than we think.

The relationship between pornography and sexual assault does exist. If some therapists believe that pornography is a positive influence in treating sexual dysfunction, then I suggest those therapists become a little more creative in their therapeutic approach.

All sex offenders have a warped perception of women. Let's not continue to reinforce this belief by selling the tools of sexual assault. Usually, I'm a First Amendment freak. But if I have to choose between defending the First Amendment and protecting the rights of women and children, I am going to choose the latter every time.

CHAIRMAN WHITE: Cheryl Champion.

Cheryl Champion: pornography obsession and saturation

MS. CHAMPION: Thank you.

My name is Cheryl Champion. I have worked in the field of sexual abuse for 12 years, from 1971 to 1983. Since 1975 I have worked in Minnesota. I have chosen to work in Minnesota because we have some of the best laws in the United States for working in the field of sexual abuse if you intend to do anything about it. I have been involved with the Minnesota Coalition of Sexual Assault programs which represented 37 statewide programs and have been a member of the Board of Directors of the National Coalition Against Sexual Assault, representing programming across the United States. I have lectured on many of the issues relating to sexual abuse, most recently the relationship between pornography and sexual violence, so it is most appropriate that I was asked to testify today. I am willing to tell you what I have personally observed in my clinical work with the victims and offenders involved in sexually violent crimes.

I am currently employed by Washington County Human Services, Inc., as part of their Sexual Abuse Unit. My colleagues and I are responsible for a multifaceted program that provides 24-hour crisis intervention and advocacy to victims, individual therapy and support group counselling to victims and their families, and an intervention program for juvenile sex offenders, and a treatment program for families involved in the behavior of incest. I do this to acquaint you with my experience in the field so that you can understand what I have to say.

CHAIRMAN WHITE: Excuse me, you said also families who are involved in incest?

MS. CHAMPION: Yes.

CHAIRMAN WHITE: Okay.

MS. CHAMPION: I would first like to comment on the incidents in which we have seen a direct relationship between pornography and the crime. Although I am opposed to telling horror stories, I think this is a time and place where this is appropriate. I can tell you about a young married woman who we saw, whose husand had the house so filled with his collections of pornography, she was too embarrassed to allow her in-laws or her family to come in. She finally came to us for help when she was left hanging upside down in the bedroom, even though the baby was crying and in need of nursing.

The second case I will tell you about is the kidnap of two young junior

111

high school women in my county who were kidnapped on their way from school and taken out into the woods and held captive overnight by a young man who had constructed a very interesting tree fort in which he had papered the walls with pornography, and spent two hours assaulting these two 14-year old girls following illustrations from the pornographic magazines that he had collected.

The third one I will tell you about is a gang of juveniles who papered the attic to their parents' garage with pornographic magazines. They kidnapped an eight-year-old neighborhood girl and gang-raped her.

They are not pleasant stories, they are not the only stories we hear. I do not tell them to horrify people but to state that pornography is clearly connected with sexual assaults that we work with. It is not uncommon for our victims to speak of the pornography involved in their assaults when giving testimony to law enforcement and in the court and in processing the incident in their therapy with us. I am continually amazed that when we have public hearings like this no one bothers to ask the real experts. That is the tree top. They should contact Chief Bouza's investigators and find out just how much pornography they collect, and catalogues, every time they get a search warrant and investigate the residence of some sexual offenders.

The second point is the prevalency of pornography amongst our offenders. Because ours is an outpatient facility, the offenders we are seeing come to us while they still live in the community. We are very careful not to treat offenders that we judge to be at risk to the community, that they would act out again. We are seeing the most, if you will, inoccuous members of the offending community. The more dangerous are referred to locked in-patient facilities such as Lino Lakes and St. Peter Criminal Hospital. Even the exposers who are guilty of visual rape in that they never physically touch their victims, to the more disturbed juvenile offenders, or the incest offenders who have violated their own children, are heavily connected to pornography. Each of these individuals has an active fantasy life involving the use of pornographic materials for masturbation, fantasy contemplation, and eventual acting out of their scenarios on their victims.

One of the underlying philosophical tenacities of our program is for all offenders in treatment to clean out their homes, garages, cars, and offices of pornographic materials. We are quite clear about not rationalizing the content, everything, pin-ups, books, magazines, TV cassettes and films. They must also contract with us not to use porn during their treatment with us. There is active discussion in groups and individual therapies about the inappropriate nature of pornographic material. Those people who violate the rule are subject to group criticism and a decision by the treatment facility whether or not they will continue that treatment and evoke their probation.

Several things are clear from our work with offenders and pornographic materials. First, that porn takes over their lives to the exclusion of any other entertainment material. Some of these people have collected such a mass of pornographic material, their garages and basements are full and they can't park their cars in the garage. It is an obsessive relationship that they have with pornography.

The second is that it is a relief, a validating statement to the families of these offenders when we encourage them to clean out these collections. In some way the family has suspected all along that the porn had some connection to the inappropriate sexual behavior.

The behavioral impact of pornography can be summarized so: first of all, that all of our offenders show that they were exposed to and involved with pornograhy at a very early age.

Two, that their secretive collections are significantly higher than those we find in other populations of adolescents.

Three, when more appropriate sexual education materials are available, juveniles do not seem to need pornographic materials.

Four, that most of our offenders in psychological testing seem predisposed to violent acting-out behavior. The question then becomes, would they have chosen violent sexual acting out without the influence of porn? I am not willing to make a statement about that because we have not done research that would stand up in the community.

And five, we use porn as a tool for redefining sexual behaviour and orientation, it is clear to us that it does influence behavior. Sexual gratification from porn is a strong reinforcer. We do much work to redirect fantasy and gratification to more appropriate, less violent, object oriented self-gratification and so we are using porn as a way to hold up something that is negative to these men and teach them how to redirect their fantasies and their lives and their tempers.

The final arguments that I want to make is that I believe it is a very sexist issue that those defenders of pornography will say to you that porn is a portrayal of normal violent nature of men's sexuality. That is the most sexist statement, and that says something also about men if we are to believe that men all have a violent expression of their sexuality.

The second thing I want to talk about is the saturation issue. We will find that term in the literature is very clear if you are a reader of pornography. I have had to because of my work, that over the last 12 years pornography has become more and more violent, that the themes in it have become more and more explicit. It is in a sense as if we can't get enough of it and so once you have seen one murder, not so expicitly, you need to have more and more portrayed realistically. You will find that people become saturated and those juveniles you see starting out with low levels of magazines that simply portray nudity, quickly move on to those "how to" rape and murder magazines that are published.

The third point that I want to ask is whether or not it is that difficult for us to recognize hate. If you will flip through any of these magazines, you will notice that the central themes are racist in many of the portrayals that are of women. And the actors who are pornographers, there tends to be a difference in that often the person is portrayed as a Black person or an Oriental person or an ethnic member of a group. You will also notice that besides being a racist, there are a lot of themes of violence such as Nazi prison camps, people who are held against their will and held powerless. It is a literature of hate and that is not very hard to understand if you were to look at it.

The fourth thing I want to say is that I have seen a percentage growth and a change in the people who are my victims. Twelve years ago when I did this work, most of the people I dealt with, it looked like the women in this room. They were white and middle-class and fairly well educated. That has changed. The majority of the vicitms I see now are children.

The other change I have noticed is, there was a percentage increase in what I call child pornography. The explicit portrayal of children being sexual with each other or adults. I think I can directly correlate that with the increase in the number of child victims I see.

The fifth thing I would say is, whether or not porn causes violent acts to be perpetrated against women is not really the question. Porn is already a violent act against women. It is our mothers, our daughters, our sisters, and our wives that are for sale for pocket change at the news-stands in this country.

The last thing I would like to say is that porn does not exist in isolation, it is not just in sleazy neighborhoods. You need to know that the gang rape in the bar in Massachusetts which gained so much notoriety was portrayed many months earlier in one of the top-selling magazines in this country as a pornographic picture outline.

The central division is between the sense of rape as an act of hostility and violence as women see and know and experience it, and rape as an erotic act as fantasized by men and practised by some. That is a direct quote from a feminist writer who I think elucidates it very clearly.

In closing I want to commend this public body for having the courage to hear this sort of testimony and encourage you to maintain your convictions in the face of those who would see this as no threat to our community. I would urge you to vote for the safety and dignity of your citizens, those you are elected to represent. Thank you.

CHAIRMAN WHITE: Ms. Champion, are there other reports from police, say in Washington County, that show when they do arrests in homes what kind of material —

MS. CHAMPION: Yes.

CHAIRMAN WHITE: Do you have — are there persons that could come and speak, right here in this department?

MS. CHAMPION: Would you like me to leave a list of names or —

CHAIRMAN WHITE: Yes, I would.

MS. CHAMPION: Okay.

CHAIRMAN WHITE: Okay, the next speaker.

Gary Kaplan: predicting possibilites of assault

MR. KAPLAN: Gary Kaplan. I have not really prepared anything to say. I am the Executive Director of Alpha Human Services, which is an inpatient treatment program for sex offenders. It's the only community-based in-patient program specifically for sex offenders in the country. There is a handful of in-patient programs, although most are within some

114

type of institution.

I am also the Director of Outpatient Treatment Programming for Sex Offenders and a licensed psychologist. I have a private practice. As part of my private practice I do a great deal of court-ordered psychological evaluations. I am currently, for instance, doing five court-ordered psychological evaluations that are on my calendar already.

I don't have a prepared speech. On the other hand, I have a number of years of experience with criminal sex offenders, probably about 10. I was an adviser to the only private psychologist with male sex offenders for a period of five years. I would like to say a few things about my observations. Unfortunately, all of us that are here that are working with criminal sex offenders lack hard data to say exactly what percentage of sex offenders are linked in some way to pornography. Yet most of my colleagues, I think, feel as I do. That clinically our impression is that there is a substantial role that pornography plays, certainly with virtually all sexually obsessed or preoccupied individuals that we see, whether committing sex crimes or not, pornography seems to be a pretty major role.

I have heard a number of people talk and it really is true, I always get the police reports and everything else when I am doing a court order. And over and over again I end up seeing they, with a search warrant, pulled out boxes of pornography. I am doing a court ordered psychological evaluation for Scott County right now, normally I have two actually in progress at the same time, and pornography played a role in that. Showing pornographic materials to 15-year old girls and getting them drugged in exchange for allowing them to engage in sexual conduct.

CHAIRMAN WHITE: Sir, are they movies or magazines or what?

MR. KAPLAN: In this particular incident they were videotapes. The psychological evaluation I just finished for Hennepin County, for Judge Schiefelbein, actually they were magazines, boxes of magazines and videotapes. Incidentally, that evaluation just went in the mail yesterday, it is really recent. The sex offender had been arrested in an adult bookstore for soliciting sex. He was anally penetrating his son, 12-year-old son, with his penis and also a son, 15 years old, from another marriage.

Another way that we see pornography being used in the commission of crimes is showing them to kids. I remember an interesting case in which an ice cream man, a Good Humor Man, always kept an open magazine by him as he drove along and the kids would look at it. And he would use that as some kind of a manipulative technique to involve the people into talking about sex or getting interested in sex. As a comment: have you ever seen anything like this before or have you ever done anything like this previously? So, you know, there is certainly a number of ways that pornographic materials are used. You know written pornography is just as troublesome as, if not more so, and it would be a lot easier for us in doing treatment with people if pornographic material weren't around. But in a lot of respects, the written pornographic materials are as troublesome as those that are graphic or pictorial.

We recently — by the way, in our programs we don't allow any

115

pornographic materials whatsoever. To my knowledge most of the other programs, of which there is two other in-patient programs in Minnesota, the treatment program in Lino Lakes and one down in St. Peter, to my knowledge, I can't say for sure, they don't allow pornographic materials to be used. At least I am sure they discourage the use of pornographic materials.

At any rate we recently found a fellow reading a book. But it is illegal taking pictures of or soliciting one under the age of 18, you know, for the purpose of engaging in obscene works. It is illegal, but it does not seem to be difficult for sex offenders to become aroused simply by reading photographically detailed stories about deviant sexual behavior or child molesting or something like that.

MS. MacKINNON: Mr. Kaplan, could you say from your clinical experience, do you see any relationship that you have observed between what the people you treat choose to look at in terms of pornography and what they actually do?

MR. KAPLAN: Yes. And I have said that a number of times to different audiences. You can't say that if you find an individual who, let's say, has pornographic materials depicting children, you know, I can't say with certainty that that person is going to engage in that behaviour but I can certainly talk in terms of probabilities. And I feel that there is an increased possibility that, in fact, that individual can be seen at some time in the future to engage in that activity. Of course, common sense will tell you, you know, people read pornographic materials for the most part to attain some type of sexual arousal or sexual feelings. And so common sense would suggest that somebody wants to look at pictures involving children engaging in some kind of sexual behavior, and that at least to him that that sexual fantasy represents the hope for reality.

Maybe I should mention a little bit about that role. There are two schools of thought, that in fact deviant sexual fantasy is an outlet, or enforcer. For those of us, certainly my colleagues, I have been doing this for 10 years, there is absolutely no doubt in my mind that masturbation, the deviant sexual fantasy, reinforces and increases the probability that that behaviour will recur as opposed to decreasing, as it would become an outlet.

I remember many years ago, we really may have been the first to take that position and I don't know of too many treatment programs that are still encouraging people to masterbate to deviant fantasy. So, if you look at sexual fantasy as a hope for reality, if you look at masturbation or climax as a reinforcer, it hardly could be considered punishment. You can see what we are doing is, we are pairing deviant sexuality with pleasurable sexual feelings — which is problematic.

Offenders have an attachment between a particular sexual stimuli, a deviant sexual stimuli or activity, and pleasurable sexual feeling. And an analogy is that many men or women may find that they become sexually aroused when they go out with somebody that wears a certain type of perfume or they smell a certain type of perfume, and without a doubt you can usually trace that and there is some positive early sexual experiences

116

or encounters with someone who, say for a woman, someone who she really cared about and felt very good about with a particular cologne that that man wore. And there is a condition kind of attachment.

Of course, that is our concern with pornographic materials because they are used as a stimulant and what it does is, it pairs positive sexual feelings with deviant stimuli, and particularly with those who are somewhat backward sexually or at a young age and they are just learning.

MS. MacKINNON: In deviance, do you include something like battery or rape?

MR. KAPLAN: Well, a sexual behaviour —

MS. MacKINNON: We are trying to be brief here, I don't mean for you to go on.

MR. KAPLAN: In diagnosing sexual deviance, look at the target of sexual behavior, the type of rape is a certain way of deviant type of sexual behavior, or you look at the motive of sexual behavior

MS. MacKINNON: Thank you.

CHAIRMAN WHITE: Thank you.

MR. KAPLAN: I don't think I was through.

CHAIRMAN WHITE: I am glad she said it because it was coming.

MR. KAPLAN: Well, I support the ordinance. I can't say whether it is going to have a preventative effect. I do know that will make my life a whole lot easier in treating sex offenders. Criminal sex offenders will go to great lengths to get pornographic materials. If they are not accessible, it would make my life a lot easier.

CHAIRMAN WHITE: Thank you. Nancy Steele.

Nancy Steele: rehearsal for assault

MS. STEELE: Thank you.

For 12 years I have worked in prisons in Colorado and Minnesota providing direct clinical treatment services to men convicted of sex offenses, rape, incest, and child molesting. For years I've heard them talk in depth about their feelings about themselves, their crimes and their sexuality. These are my own personal professional opinions I have formed in listening to them over the years on the relationship between their crimes and pornography. I also want to say that some of my opinions are based on research that I did for my doctorate.

At that time I was trying to research fantasy, this is a nonpublished dissertation. I started out with that new idea of catharsis. And I used violent offenders in a fairly complicated design. And the net result showed the opposite of what I had predicted, and was consistent with all the other literature and research I had read for my dissertation, that the angry fantasies increased anger in the offenders. What was of particular importance was that it increased it most in the most violent offenders, the most sadistic offenders.

What I want to say about a sex offender and what I have learned about them, is that they are a long time in the making. It doesn't happen suddenly with no cause. There are always long-standing background

117

reasons for their crimes and generally triggers in their current emotional environment that bring about the crimes. Pornography is both a cause and an effect of their emotional problems and very frequently plays a major part in their assaults on women and children. They generally will increase their consumption of pornography prior to sex offenses. They will get very specific ideas in reading pornography of exactly what they will do in their crimes, to whom they will do it in their crimes.

Certain types of them live years of their life in a fantasy world, isolated from real human relationships. They don't have emotional pairing relationships with other people, they don't have positive messages and values of sexuality, they don't see sexuality as a loving expression of things. What they see in their homes and what they read and what they hear in the media, is what they tend to believe about sexuality.

One man said to me just last week in group, he had been molesting his daughter over and over and over and he knew it was wrong. And he felt terrible and hated himself but he said, "I read about it in a magazine, I read how children really like this, how they want their fathers to abuse them. I knew it wasn't right but it gave me the excuse I needed to keep on doing it." They turned to pornography as a way to sort of satiate an appetite that grows in themselves. It doesn't satiate them, it is like drinking salt water. The more they drink the more they need, the more they have to seek to get what they believe they deserve.

For very lonely, very disturbed, angry men, pornography is a way in which they practice their crimes of sexual assault. They read stories, watch movies, and masturbate to angry, destructive stories of rape and degradation. Over and over they pair their fantasies with masturbation, ejaculation, and sexual release. Through a very basic conditioning process their sexual response becomes conditioned to anger, violence, and shame. Some reach the point where they cannot feel sexual feelings in a loving and respectful context with women they care about. Fantasy is not harmless for many people, certainly not all, but for many people fantasy leads to action.

I do not believe that pornography would make abusers out of most men. Most men are as disgusted by sadistic pornography as most women are. We have to recognize that there are all too many men who live very lonely, unhappy lives and for whom pornography is like a loaded gun. There are also a lot of adolescent girls and boys who are very curious about sexuality who are willing to try dangerous or forbidden things and they too are vulnerable to the ideas, messages, and feelings in pornography.

So, we have to ask ourselves as a society, just what values do we believe in? What message do we want to give to people about violence and sexuality? Why are we condoning and in some ways supporting the very sick, destructive proliferation of materials that can only harm other human beings?

I don't believe that the offender is here today that I had asked to come. He may have had trouble with the weather, is he here? No, I guess not.

MS. HOYT: I would like to ask you a question, based on your

professional life. Is it fair to say that the men you work with use violent pornographic materials as they are feeling these feelings of anger and frustration and self-loathing? Because, you know it is awfully hard to separate out erotic material.

MS. STEELE: Right.

MS. HOYT: I mean, it isn't hard for me. I know what I think is erotic and I know what I think is dangerous, because a woman in a sexual pose who is there without any whips and chains is erotic. Somebody tied to a bed with blood running out of their nose and mouth is violent.

I was wondering, did you ever get into what kinds? I would guess it would be violent stuff?

MS. STEELE: For the violent rapist they tend to use violent material. Child molesters use child pornography. I am not against erotic or sexual literature. We use it to condition child molesters to be turned on by adult sexuality. I am against sexuality which is portrayed in a degrading or violent context.

MS. HOYT: Thank you.

CHAIRMAN WHITE: Now, the next speaker is Michael O'Brien.

Are there people in the hall? If they are, have them come in especially if they are speakers.

Michael O'Brien?

UNIDENTIFIED SPEAKER: He is not in the hall.

CHAIRMAN WHITE: Not in the hall, okay.

Richelle Lee: attitudes of sex offenders

MS. LEE: I am Richelle Lee, I work with sex offenders. I work with the State of Minnesota, Department of Corrections in Oak Park Heights currently, and I also worked at Lino Lakes for one year. I recently have been establishing a sex offender porgram at Oak Park Heights. I have also worked extensively with victims in sexual family abuse.

Basically I would validate most of the comments made by other sex offender therapists. So I will keep myself brief for your benefit and mine.

I have yet to work with an offender that does not use pornography. I have had a number of offenders who made the statement that pornography, they believe for themselves, was directly responsible for where they got their ideas. Very early in their lives they were exposed to pornography and that these messages and images about women, about what sexuality is, this is where they got their education. And they believe that that exposure early in their life had a direct effect upon them as to why they then acted out later on.

Offenders that I work with in the Department of Corrections said the pornography is for sale, insofar as *Playboy, Penthouse, Screw* magazine and other contraband magazines that are sold by the prison itself in the commissary. I think the sale of pornography right there happens to condone it, our society is condoning those images and messages about women.

I spend hours in groups a day with men discussing their attitudes about

119

women, their beliefs about sexuality. They in fact fit stereotypically with those images of women: that they like to be raped, that they like to be beaten, they are very open about that. They find it difficult to change those ideas and opinions after spending hours in a group, they go back to their cells where they read the magazines and have their pin-ups on the walls.

I think the sale of pornography, at least from my perspective, has increased when any grocery store I walk in, any gas station I walk in, is selling those magazines. There is something terribly wrong with the fact that our bodies can be sold as a commodity on any shelf, that most of the magazines I know in one store I visit quite regularly are on the bottom shelf where any child, even though there are plastic covers on those, any child can see those.

The incest women that I worked with report that they were shown pictures of pornography by their uncles or fathers or aggressors to show them how it was done, that this is in fact what they were about, what they were for, and that this is okay.

Basically I will just validate the rest of what has been said and I think that the overuse of pornography and the frequent selling of it and the readily availableness of it is, let's not have it. Thank you.

CHAIRMAN WHITE: I thank you for making it brief because there are quite a few people who have signed up, some who signed up last night that didn't get a chance to speak and also are here again tonight. But we will get to you.

Paul Gerber from Hennepin County Bureau of Criminal Apprehension?

MS. DWORKIN: He doesn't seem to be here.

CHAIRMAN WHITE: Okay. Charlotte Kasl?

Charlotte Kasl: pornography as sexual addiction

MS. KASL: I am Charlotte Kasl, I am a therapist in private practice. I work with adult women survivors of sexual abuse as well as children of these survivors and the families. I also come from a — I have been doing therapy for about seven years with the victims and survivors.

I want to make two points. Basically I want to connect pornography as sexual addiction and I want to connect sexual addiction to childhood sexual abuse. I also want to say I am just terrified talking here, I don't know when I have been so scared speaking about something as this issue. I think it is loaded emotionally, it is hard to stay focused on the issues. I hear about it so much because I work with abuse.

It has been my experience that pornography is an integral part of sexual addiction and sexual addiction is an integral part of child abuse. And as these are addictions, they follow a course of escalation. They follow a course of compulsion. They are out of control. The addict using pornography is on a spiral, on a course that is getting worse, that leads to escalation of the sexual acting out whether it be peeping Tom, whether it be molesting children, exposing himself and so forth. I think by opening

120

up this issue about pornography and sexuality and sexual addiction, we are going to open up the whole area around child abuse, and around the way we need to redefine what is sexual instead of what is violence.

All children who live in the home, this is my opinion, all children who live in the home of a sexual addict at some level become victims of that addiction. And that person does not have to bring pornography home for that to happen. The energy that person carries, the fantasies, the thoughts, the way they talk and look at their female children communicates something about this child to their bodies. Young girls talk about, "I couldn't stand it when my father touched me, there was something wrong." Some direct connections I have talked about with clients and they said they were glad to have the stories here, they felt it was so important.

One example, for instance, was a young girl by the age of four. She saw her parents sitting on the couch together reading pornographic magazines. When she tried to go join them they were laughing and happy. She said it was the only time she saw her father's eyes light up, he felt alive. When she tried to read they said "No, no," which was confusing because they seemed happy reading this.

By five years old this young woman, at that time a young girl, would bring boys from the neighborhood, draw off her clothes the way she had seen in the magazines and let herself be abused sexually. This is by five years old.

This woman has gone through a great deal of work. She was alcoholic, very ill. She is now a student, she is now working through these things in therapy and is recovering, but she had never herself made the connection to the pornography. All she felt about herself: she was crazy, she was sick. How at five years old could I have been doing this?

Pornography in the home is insidious. Girls pick up the message, they act it out, they don't know why they feel suicidal and crazy. I have seen this many, many times.

Another example I would like to share with you was a little boy I worked with, whose father was preoccupied with pornography and had a house full of it. The little boy was known at school as the kisser. He would jump at girls, grab them and kiss them. He was already developing an abuser mentality by the age of six. This happens to children, again, without them knowing it. He wanted to be like his father, that is what his father liked. He was doing what every child will do. It models for children that sexuality has power, and that women are basically pieces of meat.

A third example was in a very abusive, violent family where the father had read a great deal of pornography. It was kept in his room and the children knew it was there. He beat his children a lot, his daughters particularly. The girls used to sneak in when the parents were gone, read the pornography. They became addicted to it, it was their only escape as it had been their father's escape.

The woman that reported it, today at 30 is addicted to pornography, has yet to have intimate sexual relationships or free herself from the connection of silence and sexuality. I think the growing use of 12 step groups for sexual addicts and co-addicts in the City of Minneapolis will say that the awareness here is growing extremely quickly and we have a lot to be proud of, that we are opening up the issues.

Another woman with a battering father, she saw her father read a great deal of pornography. She came away imprinted in her mind that all her father was interested in was sex which generalized too that men must always be interested in sex and no men can be trusted. When she was around them she thought, what is my father thinking of me. In both these cases, the fathers were silent with the daughters. I believe a lot of battering of young girls has to do with sexual feelings, much of what comes every time in families where there was pornography. The father feels sexual towards his daughter, wants to repress that and instead of taking responsibility for his addiction, which is out of his control, beats his daughter. It is connected many times. I have had fathers open up to this when they come to family therapy and talk about it.

Myself, I was in therapy some years back. I walked into a drug store and saw my therapist reading a pornographic magazine; I actually froze in my tracks. I felt so abused. In therapy with this man I always thought, "What is he thinking of me, what is he thinking when he sees my body?" I know the feelings I had were those children had. This was a trusted person I put my faith into, and I never could get past it. And I, at that time, didn't know enough or didn't have the feeling to speak, just as a child doesn't know enough to speak, they don't have the ability. They believe whatever goes on at home must be normal. These things are imprinted to children, they are dangerous to children.

The last example is going into a local grocery store there to return grapefruit. There was in the back room a picture of a naked woman from the back with a little diagram saying rump, ribs, shoulder, like they do with cows. I was upset. The first time I saw it I couldn't talk. I came back later, walked in and saw it again. I was incredibly amazed that the store could have this, this is damaging. I said to the man, "I find this offensive, returning white grapefruit for pink ones and standing there with my daughter, that my daughter is a piece of meat and her mother is a piece of meat." He finally took it down.

The fact is that we need to wake people up. I think Minneapolis has an incredible opportunity to put themselves on the map as a very strong forerunner in these liberties for women and making us feel free, to make us not feel we are violated and not see ourselves as meat.

CHAIRMAN WHITE: Thank you.

MS. MacKINNON: Chairman White, I would like to submit a couple of documents now from Minneapolis that are in the same vein as the testimony that was just given. I will not read them.

CHAIRMAN WHITE: Thank you.

MS. MacKINNON: The first is from the Family Nurturing Center. I will note, in it children are exposed to pornography and this can include child pornography and adult pornography, even the exposure in that way leads to people responding in later life at that time as if they were actual incest victims.

122

I am also submitting a letter to the City Council, from the Kiel Clinics in Minneapolis, talking about the use of pornography in the abuse of children and adult women.

And a letter from VOICE, Incorporated, which is a national organization for victims of incest, to the City Council talking about the place of pornography in incest. And all of these letters are expressing support for this ordinance.

CHAIRMAN WHITE: Okay. Joan Webster?
Sue Santa:?

Sue Santa: coercion into prostitution with pornography

MS. SANTA: I am Sue Santa, I work with a local non-profit private organization in Minneapolis called Minneapolis Youth Division. My position there is outreach worker, working exclusively with adolescent females involved in prostitution. Over the course of the years, six years that I have been there, I noticed a direct correlation between pornography and prostitution with my clients. I can say almost categorically, never have I had a client who has not been exposed to prostitution through pornography in one way or the other.

For some young women that means that they are shown pornography, either films, videotapes, or pictures, as "This is how you do it," almost as a training manual in how to perform acts of prostitution.

CHAIRMAN WHITE: Excuse me, you are saying they are pimps training them with those kind of messages?

MS. SANTA: That is correct.

In addition, out on the street when a young woman is plying her trades as it were, many of her tricks or customers will come up to her with little pieces of paper, pictures that were torn from a magazine and say, "I want this." As one client put it, it is like a mail order catalogue of sex acts, and that is what she is expected to perform.

Another way that pornography plays a part in the lives of my clients is that as young women, very young women — some as young as 11 — they want the good things that are to be had in the United States, they want the kinds of things that they see on TV, and they see taking part in nude modelling, taking part in movies, pornographic movies, as a way to be a star, get to Hollywood. Now this may seem foolish to those of you who are adults and say "Ha ha, we know that is wrong." We are talking about children who are very naive and are told that Marilyn Monroe made it this way, Brooke Shields made a movie about *Pretty Baby,* "you have been there baby, you can do it."

Another aspect that plays a big part in my work with my clients is that on many occasions my clients are multi, many rape victims. These rapes are often either taped or have photographs taken of the event. The young woman, when she tries to escape or leaves, is told that either she continues in her involvement in prostitution or those pictures will be sent to her parents, will be sent to the juvenile court, will be used against her. And out of fear she will continue her involvement in prostitution.

123

On several occasions, not many but on several occasions, these young women have found that later their pictures have been published in pornographic magazines without their knowledge and consent. This is very traumatic, especially when I have been working hard with this young woman to make things in her life better. She is involved in the straight life style and finds out there are published pictures of her engaged in various sex acts.

I would like to close with a comment of one of my clients who heard I was going to be here tonight who said, "It is about time that those folks figured out what is going on." Thank you.

Sherry Arndt: use of pornography to confuse child abuse victims

MS. ARNDT: My name is Sherry Arndt, and I am a moderator and trainer with the Illusion Theater here in Minneapolis. The Illusion Theater is a theater based in Minneapolis which has, since 1977, had a child sexual abuse prevention program as part of its theater.

Many people I think are probably aware of our existence and some of the work that we do. We perform two plays, one called *Touch* which is for elementary students and helps explain to children what the difference is between good and bad touch and what they can do when they are confused by touch.

Our second play is called *No Easy Answers* and it is for a teen-age audience and helps — it covers the material presented in *Touch* and enlarges on that to cover as well as images in advertising, sexual decision making, acquaintance rape, and incest and other pertinent information that is interesting to teen-agers.

We also do numerous workshops for parents, community groups and professional groups on the area of child sexual abuse prevention. We have performed in over 35 states to over 280,000 people.

My only background is as public health nurse. I worked for 11 years in public school systems, nine of those years serving as a founder and representative on our county's child abuse team.

Our two plays are based on research done in the Minneapolis public schools with school children. They are based and also use the actual comments of children in the plays as well as comments from victims, comments from offenders, and some of the actors who corroborated on the plays' own experiences.

And in a recently published major study of child sexual abuse by David Finkelhor, who is a major researcher, in a major study published, one of the reasons that children gave for why they did not report that they had been sexually abused was that they were confused by the offender's insistence that the sexual behavior was normal and that other people liked the activity.

One of the most common ways that offenders do convince children is that the sex is normal and pleasurable or should be pleasurable is through showing them pornographic pictures of other children engaged in sex acts looking as though they enjoy it. This is also one of the main ways that

124

offenders coerced children into posing for pornographic photographs, is by showing them other pictures of other children and saying, "Well, everybody else likes it. There must be something wrong with you if you don't find this pleasant," and "Gee, you know you liked it the last time we were together." Offenders are very seductive with children.

In all of our work, and as I said we travel extensively, we see over and over again a confusion that exists between what is okay and what is not okay in the whole area of sex between what is sexuality and what is violence. This confusion is brought about in large part by pornography as well as other images in our culture that confuse us about what we are supposed to be like and what other people are like and how we are supposed to act. In fact, this is so pervasive that I think the influence of pornography has seeped into other written material that most of us don't consider pornography.

I brought with me a couple of examples of that: the December issue of *Harper's Bazaar* which shows an eight-year old girl in a perfume ad. She is dressed seductively, the photograph has made sure that her nipples are exposed. Part of the copy in this article is "Jasmine and Gardenia for seduction, with just a hint of innocence. Dreams of far away places synonymous with elegance, the height of confident femininity." I think it is not difficult for any of us to see the influence of pornography in this magazine article.

I also have another article from the December issue of *Vogue* which shows a photograph of a woman elegantly dressed in evening wear, fondling a naked, about 14-year-old boy. The caption on this is, "Age makes no difference". Neither magazine would probably be identified by most of us as pornographic. So much confusion exists in our culture about the differences between sexuality and violence that we are currently working on a third dramatic piece that will be for adult audiences, and it will specifically focus on the confusion between sexuality and violence that exists in our culture.

When society sanctions violence, especially violent use of sex against women and children, this attitude and resulting behavior begin to be defined as normal and natural. I think we have heard testimony to that over and over again today. I don't think I need to give any examples of that here.

When healthy sexual attitudes are prohibited by society, they begin to be defined as unnormal and unnatural. Sexuality and violence are used in our culture to the point tha they are not separated in our minds, nor are they separated in our behaviors.

It is my position that we must separate sexuality and violence. This ordinance certainly speaks toward a good beginning to do that. We must accept the normality of seuality and the seeking of pleasure, or we will see increase in individual and group violence. Thank you.

CHAIRMAN WHITE: Thank you.

Christopher Street representative?

MS. MacKINNON: I think they said they were unable to make it.

CHAIRMAN WHITE: Okay. Sue Schafer?

Sue Schafer: pornography as instruction manual for abuse

MS. SCHAFER: My name is Sue Schafer, I am a psychologist in a private practice. And over the last eight years I would say at least half of my clients have been physically or sexually abused. I just arrived and I don't have the history to know what has been addressed.

The point I would like to make is similar to the previous speaker, Sue Santa, who talked about how pornography is used as training guides. While Sue talked about how the underworld often uses it to solicit young ladies for prostitution, I would like to talk about how pornography is used by acquaintances or family members, again as guidelines or as recipe books.

CHAIRMAN WHITE: It seems to me since 1:30 of yesterday that I have been hearing more and more, it seems to be that the family structure is a part of the problem. And could you speak to that?

MS. SCHAFER: Well, I think the example that I am planning to use may address that.

I would like to state three present or near present cases that I am working with, where family members or acquaintances have used pornography as recipe books. Presently or recently I have worked with clients who have been sodomized by broom handles, forced to have sex with over 20 dogs in the back seat of their car, tied up and then electrocuted on their genitals. These are children or in the ages of 14 to 18, all of whom I could have found a direct impact by pornography, either where the perpetrator has read the manuals and manuscripts at night and used these as recipe books by day, or had the pornography present at the time of sexual violence.

And so as the previous speaker talked about the importance of separating sex and violence, I recognize, I think any step to take or eliminate pornography would be a step in the direction of separating out sex and violence.

Another further complication I see in working with the clients as children, once these children grow up into adults there becomes a tremendous link between sex and violence, so much so that in their mind that sadomasochistic behaviors are something they fight, oftentimes on a daily basis. For these children that grow up and become adults, oftentimes sex becomes impossible without some form of self-mutilation or violence. So while it is directly connected with their adult sexual activity, it is also connected in a general sense with self-mutilating types of behaviors that continue. Thank you.

CHAIRMAN WHITE: Thank you very much.

MS. MacKINNON: Chairman White, I would like to submit a few documents at this time.

CHAIRMAN WHITE: Okay.

MS. MacKINNON: I would also offer a brief interpretation of the evidence, in answer to your question. Perhaps one way to think about what we have heard about family is that we have illustrated that the family is no exception to the abuses that exist of women and children throughout this society.

The documents I would like to submit, the first three are by writers, each of whom has submitted a statement to the Minneapolis City Council on the occasion of the consideration of this ordinance. They are all writers in the area of incest and child abuse.

The first is by Trudee Able-Peterson who wrote the book *Children of the Evening* which is looking at child prostitution in America.

The second is by Katherine Brady who wrote the book *Father's Days*. And she brings up a statement about her own particular experience of incest and how pornography plays in that as well as other accounts from her knowledge of the subject.

The third is a letter from Louise Armstrong who wrote the book *Kiss Daddy Goodnight,* a speakout on incest. She wrote a letter and extensive statement to the Minneapolis City Council connecting her research on incest with pornography.

A fourth letter to the Minneapolis City Council comes from "Incest Survivors Resource Network International" from New York who enthusiastically endorses your efforts in bringing the relationship of incest and pornography to a public forum.

CHAIRMAN WHITE: Let the record show.

Floyd Winecoff?

MS. MacKINNON: He is unable to come.

CHAIRMAN WHITE: Michael Laslett?

Michael Laslett: men's fantasies and actions controlled by pornography

MR. LASLETT: My name is Michael Laslett. Before I read my own statement, I would like to read a statement of a psychologist by the name of Floyd Winecoff who was unable to be here this evening. He has been working with men for many years. The title of his statement is "Pornography and its Effects on Men."

"My expertise in addressing this subject somes from a 10-year psychotherapy practice specializing in services for men. My practice has included over the years an ongoing treatment group for men who are physically, verbally, or sexually abusive. I have repeatedly found a direct link between pornography and attitudes towards women as objects that contribute to the ongoing crime of violence against women.

"The myth about pornography is that is frees the libido and gives men an outlet for sexual expression which liberates mind and body. This is truly myth. I have found that pornography not only does not liberate men, but on the contrary becomes a source of bondage. Men masturbate to pornography only to become addicted to the fantasy. There is no liberation for men in pornography. Pornography becomes a source of addiction much like alcohol. there is temporary relief. It is mood altering. And it is reinforcing, i.e. 'you want more' because 'you got relief'. It is this reinforcing characteristic that leads men to want the experience which they have in photographic fantasy to happen in 'real' life.

"An endless search ensues to capture the docile woman of fantasy in total real life availability. The more hopeless it is to find this sort of woman, the more desperate becomes the interaction between men and the women they pursue.

"The problem arises when real women do not like being dominated, controlled, and 'made love to' on one sided terms. When women assert themselves, men experience a loss of the feeling of being in control. Violence occurs in men when their own personal concept of 'masculinity' is challenged. A man who is already addicted to the feeling of needing to have sex, and the fantasy of being in control, becomes desperate in his behavior when confronted by a woman who doesn't want what's being given out.

"Women lose and men lose too. Women lose, of course, because they are the object of this abusive pursuit. Men lose becuse they never experience true intimacy that comes from letting down and opening up with someone. Many men let down and open up when there is a threat of losing the relationship; but violence is a more common occurence.

"There is no social communion in domination and control. By nature we are social beings, and as such require true social interaction for well-beingness. Without such social communion, there exists only isolation and desperation.

"Pornography portrays a fantasy of social communion, but in reality it contributes to the desperation that leads men to abusivenes. There is no difference between the person who will lie, steal, cheat, or kill in order to get the drug or chemical of addicted choice. Pornography is the chemical of sexual addiction."

And my own statement. I have been raised and socialized in a pornographic society. Pornographic images of women have surrounded and bombarded me throughout my life; images which depict women primarily as sexual objects available to me at any time, as sexually submissive, as meaning yes even when they say no, as always wanting sex, and as finding abuse sexually enjoyable.

Everywhere I go I carry a pornographic notion of what an "attractive" woman is, what she looks like, how she acts, what she says and so on. I have been infected with pornographic, sexist, and blatantly oppressive expectations of women as friends, co-workers, passers-by, lovers. My sexism, however, is not a haphazard occurrence. I am the result of a systematic socialization process which trains all men to oppress women, because it is in the interests of men as the economic, political, sexual and cultural rulers of this society to keep women down. Pornography is a crucial tool in the maintenance of male power.

While consolidating this male-supremacist system, pornography also directly harms men as individuals. For most of my life I accepted pornographic definitions of women. How large were their breasts, their buttocks, their waist. I was only attracted to women who met very narrow standards and my sense of self-worth depended, in large part, on how many such women were interested in me. But pornography portrays women as insatiable. So while, for the good of my self-image and my status in the eyes of male friends, I wanted as many women as possible attracted to me, I was also terrified of being sexually inadequate.

Even after I became aware of my sexism and its links to pornography, I couldn't simply shed a lifetime of socialization. I couldn't escape the perceptions of women I had been taught. I began to hate myself for being sexist and for finding pornography arousing.

For years I couldn't interact with a woman without feeling that I was oppressing her, especially if I found her attractive. Since physical love-making is one of the most intimate forms of interaction and since it has been so twisted and mutilated by pornography, I couldn't sleep with a woman without feeling that I was oppressing her because my attraction for her had been influenced by pornography. I am still struggling with these feelings today.

Women are assaulted daily by and because of pornography, and my life and sexuality have been warped and distorted by it. Countering these effects of patriarchy will be a lifetime endeavor. I urge you to pass this leglislation to help us in the task of dismantling our crippling pornographic images. Let us work so that women will be less oppressed, that men will be less well trained to oppress them, and that women and men will be free to live healthier and more equal lives. Thank you.

MS. DWORKIN: May I please put these documents into evidence.

I am sorry that Chairman White isn't here, he has been expressing a desire to have confirmed his perception that pornography does hurt men in a very serious way.

And we would like to end by submitting a part of a book by an author named Timothy Beneke of rape which documents the relationship between pornography and men's attitudes on rape.

And in addition, a letter from an individual named Jim Lovestar who talks about how he feels that pornography has hurt him as a man because it has genuinely decreased his intimacies. And he is from Minneapolis.

And I would also like to submit into evidence a letter from John Stoltenberg who is originally from Minneapolis who is not living here now. He is the Chair of the Antipornography Task Group of the National Organization for Men. And that group sponsors this ordinance and Mr. Stoltenberg has had a lot of experience doing workshops on pornography with men, and men find it to be extremely disorienting and disruptive to their social learning behavior. And I think that he is representing a political opposition among men to the existence of pornography. So I submit this letter also. Thank you.

MS. HOYT: Ms. Dworkin, I will tell you that we do have microphones, we do have speaker boxes back in our offices. And from time to time, as you see committee members getting up and leaving, they are not out of hearing of the hearing going on. And Chairman White, I am sure, is listening.

MS. DWORKIN: Thank you. I was concerned only because the Chairman, I think, has been very clear about his own feelings in that direction and in the course of these hearings.

MR. DAUGHTERY: Anything further? We will move on to Omar Johnson.

MS. HOYT: Mr. Chairman?

MR. DAUGHTERY: Go ahead, Charlee.

MS. HOYT: I will go ahead. I would like to reiterate the statement, the longer we are here the tireder we seem to become. As we hear all testimony tonight, either in agreement or in opposition of your feelings, I ask that you give all credence in as much don't hiss, don't boo, please let people have their say.

MR. DAUGHTERY: All right. Mr. Johnson, proceed. Give your name and address.

Omar Johnson: men's minds trapped

MR. JOHNSON: Omar Johnson, 1920 Third Avenue South, Apartment 21.

And I'm going to be talking about myself. I was raised in Ecuador on a mission compound. The school library was well censored. My sexual life began quite late. In fact I was a junior at Dartmouth College before I even masturbated. The procedure, I remember, was self-conscious, primitive, even silly. But at the moment of orgasm there was an image. I saw a green, grassy knoll out of which popped a white rabbit and it looked at me quizzically, then bounded away, cotton tail flipping through the foliage. It's an image that will always stay with me, the fertility of the rabbit, the continuing virginity of the whiteness, nothing ever lost that cannot be regained, and the green, green earth all around.

Of course, this poetry didn't last too long. I had a friend down the hall that introduced me to another bunny. It was so legitimate: an interview with Jimmy Carter and everything. The picture gave me a feeling somewhere between queasiness and arousal. I didn't know what to do or think about them. But the section where readers write in to the editor detailing their exploits solved that problem. I was a very quick study. I mean, I had already internalized messages suggesting that women were second-class creatures. I mean, I lived in a society that had applauded me when I knocked someone out on the football field and then wandered around in a daze myself for a couple of minutes.

Violence as pleasure was something I already knew. This was just another context. By the end of the year I was stringing together long involved fantasies where women did what I wanted and loved me for it.

Then — I am out of college now — I met and got involved with a real woman. She was very special in that she did not have the capacity to seem simpler than she was. It was I who would have to learn to live with and love her complexity. It has not been easy. She is very sensitive to what she calls "connectedness." I could not manage it. Trying hard to do right by her, I failed miserably, got frustrated, used to storm out of the house yelling, "What more can I give?"

I have never been physically violent with her, but there have been occasions when I got angry at her and then I found myself in an adult bookstore reading my fantasies, as I said before: women felt fear, and pleasure, and fulfilment, according to my whim.

130

But all this time, perhaps because I remembered the beauty and creativity of my first sexual image which I found very ludicrous at the time — by the way, I knew her way with sex and with love was what I wanted — my point is that if women in a society filled by pornography must be wary for their physical selves, a man, even a man of good intentions, must be wary for his mind.

My spill into pornography felt like a congenital weakness, like getting a hernia. Perhaps it is only a cultural weakness. The point is, for me, having porn around was like the freedom to fall into a trap that I have been a long time climbing out of.

I would like, very much, to get back to following the rabbit of my own dreaming. I do not want to be a mechanical goose-stepping follower of the Playboy bunny, because that is what I think it is. Porn makes me feel goose bumps as well as erections, these are the experiments a master race perpetuates on those slated for extinction.

Now the woman I live with is Jewish. She makes me think about the connection, she was very afraid after the brutal rape and beating a couple of weeks ago which happened a couple blocks from our apartment. She tried to joke about arming herself with a frying pan and was comfortable with organizing a frying pan brigade. But it was no good. She was still afraid. And just as a well-meaning German was afraid in 1933, I am also very much afraid. Thank you.

MS. C: My name is --.

CHAIRMAN WHITE: Excuse me, before you begin did we get documentation of Mr. Johnson's notes?

You may go ahead.

Ms. W: pornography as reminder of rape

MS. W: I am speaking as a resident of Minneapolis. I have lived in Minneapolis for approximately 28 years and about 20 of those have been within a six-block radius of the Lake Street area. I am presently living in the Chicago/Lake area, less than half a block from the Rialto Theater and the bookstore.

As a child, when I was growing up I experienced some good things on Lake Street. I don't know if anybody can remember, I used to go roller skating on Dupont and Lake, movies at the American and Vogue — I am just shaking — Theaters at Lyndale and Lake and the hobby shop and pet shop at Bryant and Lake.

Also in the past, I was raped by my father for over a year from six to seven years old and I witnessed the beatings of my mother through my entire childhood, through my teenage years. Also I saw the pornography literature — paperback books, black and white magazines — in my father's bedroom through the entire time of my childhood and into my teenage years until I left. I didn't know that that sexual abuse and physical abuse was wrong. I found that out about two and a half years ago, and I have been working on it ever since.

The only thing that I did know or that I felt, was that it was my fault. My struggle to stay alive is my process which I call reclaiming myself, not living out of shame.

Daily when I walk out of my house, and I would see the doors open as usual and business as usual at the Rialto Theater and the bookstore, and I go into the Marlin Gas Station to get bus change and in front of me displayed in *Hustler* magazine, "Hustler rejects" depicting a naked woman stuffed into a garbage can, legs hanging out and dismembered body parts stuffed behind her: what I see is that women's bodies are rejected. It is okay to be dismembered and they belong in a garbage can. It say to me that physical and sexual violence is okay, acceptable, in demand, and paid for. That the rape of a six-year-old girl is okay and acceptable.

I also see pornography as relying on mass production and marketing. And I see its main motive as providing sensory stimulation and gratification through extreme sexual violence, mutilation, and finally death of women and children's bodies.

This incident of my rape is but a part of the entire oppression. In the midst of this social decay that confronts each of us here, I believe there is a strong resistance growing. No longer do I need to seek recognition through the rape of my body, but that I rid myself of the fear that silences me to repossess myself. What is deadly to me is the masses which rely on this form of violent, visual expression to base their daily interaction with me as a woman.

And I publicly protest the pornography in my neighborhood, and the Chicago/Lake area and I am glad that I am able to speak here and I support this ordinance. Thank you.

CHAIRMAN WHITE: Is Joan Gilbertson in here?

Joan Gilbertson, Powderhorn Park Association

MS. GILBERTSON: My name is Joan Gilbertson. I live at 3431 11th Avenue South, which is in close proximity to the Chicago/Lake district. I am here to say for the Powderhorn Park Association, which I am a member, supports this ordinance wholeheartedly. We encourage you to pass this ordinance. Thank you.

CHAIRMAN WHITE: Thank you.

Due to the snow, there was someone that was late.

Kathleen McKay: pornography as element of a punishing culture

MS. McKAY: My name is Kathleen McKay, I am a licensed psychologist in the State of Minnesota and I am Administrator of Sagaris, a Mental Health Center for women located in South Minneapolis, for nine and a half years.

I am speaking from my experience and that of my collegues, psychologists and psychiatrists. We see women who voluntarily seek assistance for life's problems, relationships, parenting, career issues, and so on and they range in age generally from 23 to 63.

I can say without exaggeration that every woman we have seen over the last nine and a half years has sustained damage, living in a milieu which systematically presumes and teaches that women's bodies are available for the titillation of the public.

The degradation and shame spoken about by Linda Marchiano is something all women know about: catcalls on the street, copper girls on a marquee, rapes, rapes and more rapes.

Part of what I do with women in therapy must be to teach them how to compensate for this, how to live in an oppressive/punishing culture that does not teach and barely allows women to take pride in their own bodies and in themselves.

United States Supreme Court Justice William O. Douglas, during the abortion debates some time ago, wrote a brief piece relating to the right of privacy. And I quote mostly from him, he talks about the customary presumption in a free society and the freedom to walk, freedom to stroll or even loaf without being harassed. Pornography is one of the most powerful teaching aids in the socialization and training of both girls and boys, and adult women and men. The consistent and persistent presentation of women as victims is training in the notion that women are available for use, abuse, degradation, shame and disgust.

My guarantees and promises as a citizen of the United States and resident of Minneapolis dictate that I should be able to walk or stroll in my town, even Hennepin Avenue and designated Lake Street corners, without having pornographic expressions screaming shame and humiliation at me. This does offend my civil rights as they are promised to me.

I want to express my appreciation and that of my colleagues at Sagaris to Ms. MacKinnon and Dworkin for their drafting of this ordinance. Once again, putting Minneapolis on the map as a first in progressive legislation.

Also our appreciation of Alderman Hoyt and Van White for their understanding of the issue and sponsorship of this ordinance. I urge, may I say plead with you, to seriously consider this ordinance and get a workable law for Minneapolis. Thank you very much.

CHAIRMAN WHITE: Thank you.

Dick Marple?

Dick Marple: objection to sexist language in the Bill

MR. MARPLE: I am speaking as a citizen of Minneapolis. I am not affiliated with any groups and wasn't a scheduled speaker or anything like that. I have some problems with the ordinance. I think a number of the points defining what pornography is are vague and fail to distinguish between violent pornography, which I find generally reprehensible, and general erotic expression which I find enjoyable, and I think it is my right as a citizen of the United States. Particularly the subheadings on the definition that I think are quite vague are numbers one, five, six, and seven. I fail to see how a jury or a judge would be able to determine whether women are presented as whores by nature, I don't know what that means. It is a nice slogan, I don't think it is a legally significant term.

I think women presented as sexual objects, I think in any professional encounter both regardless of their gender, may be sexual objects to each other and I see that as a legitimate form of sexual expression.

I am unclear on number five, what is the posture of sexual submission, if this has to do with the positioning of the bodies or who is involved, I think that is pretty vague.

And I am not sure about number six which refers to women being reduced to these body parts. My main concern with this is that in attempting to eliminate pornography from the silent pornography in Minneapolis we may be stepping on legitimate rights of expression and people's right to enjoy themselves in a nonoffensive way. I am also appalled, in a Civil Rights ordinance, at the sexist language. It says "the sexuality of women," there is no mention of children or men and I don't believe that they should be relegated to second-class citizenship.

I would also like to say that we have a Civil Right ordinance trying to discourage presenting women as whores by nature, then I believe that men have a Civil Right not to be presented as rapists by nature. And I have read books by feminists in which they apparently describe men this way. And I believe that if you will not accept the predecessor of this law that men act out according to descriptions or portrayals, then I question some of these writers who portray men as rapists by nature. Perhaps they just assign them to silence or telling them this is what you are, you might as well do it. I think that is sick.

I am a clerk of the Minneapolis Public Library. I do not speak for the Public Library, I speak as a concerned employee. And the bottom half of my sentence is that I don't see the distinctions between violent pornography and erotic material. I believe that the library can be in deep trouble if individuals are allowed to censor the material that is in the library which would include art books, romances which are written by and for women. Such instructive material as the Bible, lives of saints, tracts and feminist matters.

I am also concerned — I am concerned that there may be restrictions, at least threatened lawsuits against news agencies who may, depending on your definition of the word graphic, when they describe a sex crime. The possibility of someone thinking the Civil Rights were violated might bring a lawsuit against a newspaper for reporting this, that defeats the purpose.

I might also point out that if this bill had been passed before 1969 we may never have known about My Lai Massacre in Vietnam because some of the photographs that we used to report this would have been considered pornographic and unlawful under this ordinance.

My concern with the subheading of section four, number one, which deals directly with public libraries, is they have to determine "open display" of pornography. We have heard a woman describe *Vogue* magazine, *Harper's Bazaar* as having pornographic images in it. I don't believe the library has the funds to defend each and every item they have.

MS. HOYT: Mr. Chairman, I am sorry for interrupting, I would like to call your attention in the ordinance on the second page, under the discrimination of trafficking in pornography, number one, which says,

"City, state and federally funded libraries or private and public university and college libraries in which pornography is available for study shall not be construed to be trafficking in pornography but open display of pornography in said places is sex discrimination."

MR. MARPLE: Is open display circulating a copy of a book that is on a shelf so someone can see the cover? That is not very clear to me.

MS. HOYT: I wanted to make sure —

MR. MARPLE: I have been stewing about it for five days.

I also question section seven, which is on the back page of the ordinance, in which it refers to assault and battery due to pornography. Any person, which I think should be used in the previous section in pornography instead of women, who is assaulted or battered in a way that is directly caused by specific pornography has a claim, et cetera; if you refer to an act as having been directly caused by a specific piece of pornography, are you not absolving the perpetrator from guilt?

MR. HYATT: Would you move back?

MR. MARPLE: Are you not absolving the perpetrator from guilt as a result of pornography? You are denying this person free will and therefore I wonder if he can be a prosecutor. I think the most dangerous part of the ordinance —

MS. MacKINNON: I am sorry, I really missed what you said about assault and battery. What was the initial criticism?

MR. MARPLE: I objected to the phrase "directly caused by specific pornography" because to me it seems to remove responsibility.

MS. MacKINNON: That isn't what I meant. What I didn't understand is, I will tell you what I seem to understand from what you said before, that there was something wrong in saying man, child or transsexual?

MR. MARPLE: Yeah. I was referring back to the section that defines pornography. I think a person or human being would cover all categories.

MS. MacKINNON: Obviously you are saying that to you it would be an improvement to state that in that summary form rather than the specific categories of persons?

MR. MARPLE: Yeah, I think so. I think that would cover everybody. And I think in the definition under the ordinance using the word women, instead of people, or men, children, transsexual, anybody else you want to include seems discriminatory in a Civil Rights ordinance. I think there should be as much concern against violence for women and children and men as there is for women.

MS. HOYT: Are you aware, the reason there is a Civil Rights ordinance is because it is women who have been, as a class, placed in this subordination second-class position and that is why it is a Civil Rights issue, that is why it says women so often? Children are mentioned here and not mentioned elsewhere because there are already laws on the books about child pornography.

MR. MARPLE: Okay, I appreciate that. I still think men have the right also.

My major concern, and I am ready to close, is that the basic rights of expression in this country, I believe, are fundamental and I think that this ordinance prohibits more than it tends to prohibit. And I find it very difficult to accept that a writer or an artist can be prohibited from expressing himself or herself. I might add that books, organized opinions that are done with the intention of putting out abuses and injustices, would likewise be prohibited by this ordinance. And also I question if this ordinance were passed and lawsuits were taking place, whether other groups might not say that they have Civil Rights that are being violated by other things, such as I have an 87-year-old grandmother who is very religious and who I am sure thinks it is a crime against nature just even thinking about two women having sex together. And I wonder if she would have walked by the Amazon Bookstore or any place else, if her Civil Rights would not be violated.

CHAIRMAN WHITE: Is that all you have?

MR. MARPLE: That is all.

CHAIRMAN WHITE: Thank you.

MR. HYATT: Are you an attorney in a lawsuit?

MR. MARPLE: No. I am not. I am a law clerk at the library.

Jan Spring: fear generated by pornography

MS. SPRING: Hello, I am Jan Spring. I live at 3046 15th Avenue South, which is half a block away from the nearest pornography theater. And I have to say, I feel particularly privileged to speak following Mr. Marple; he addressed several of the items that I would like to address, particularly the question of free speech and so forth which has always been brought up whenever feminists raised questions about pornography.

I believe that in this ordinance, for the first time, we have a way of dealing with pornography which doesn't get us into that problem. Up until this time sexually explicit and abusive materials were dealt with in terms of obscenity.

What obscenity means to me is that sex is dirty, that my body is dirty because it is associated with sex and that I should be ashamed and that any place, any bookstore or other thing that displays women's bodies or, you know, deals in sex at all, should be relegated to certain neighborhoods which are undesirable, such as my neighborhood or such as neighborhoods in which poor men and women live or in such neighborhoods of which people of color live.

In this ordinance a distinction between simply sexual or erotic materials are not addressed by the ordinance and therefore, not prohibited. And materials which are designed to harm women to keep us in a state of submission, to keep us afraid, that latter group of material is prohibited and it doesn't depend on the neighborhood. The neighborhood I live in has been apparently for a long time considered a neighborhood where pornography is permitted; that does not go by zoning and does not go by neighborhoods and it is important that it not be permitted in somebody else's neighborhood.

Now, I am speaking as a private citizen although I have worked with sexually assaulted and battered women and I am a therapist. I have lived in Minneapolis for about four and a half years and I have chosen to live in the Powderhorn neighborhood all that time which means that for four and a half years, not every day but many days, I have stood on the bus corner in front of whatever happened to be the local closest porn shop, waiting for a bus. And I would walk by it on my way home so that I am not able to forget about the existence of pornography.

Currently I have two daughters and when they want to walk to the drugstore or to the grocery store, both of which are in walking distance and easy for them to get to, they walk by the Avalon Theater. They probably walk by that theater once or twice a day. I wonder what it does to their minds, I don't know. I spoke to my daughter, I called her to wish her a happy birthday and I asked her if anything had ever happened there. She said no, nothing particularly had ever happened there.

But I worry about my daughters because they have to go by this place. I worry about them when they have to go out to play with the other kids in the neighborhood because most of the kids in the neighborhood are boys and they are subject to the influence of pornography, which says to them that women and girls are objects and less than human. And because those boys have demonstrated that because I don't live with a man they think that my particular house is an okay house to vandalize and my guests are okay to harass, and that it is okay for them to come and break into my house just for fun to scare my daughters — this happened, it is on the police report. And, you know, when I spoke to the parents about it, that is what the boys said: it was just for fun.

So what porn means to me is that I can't forget that, what society thinks of me, which is that I am an object, I am a sex object, I am not a human being. If I ever get raped walking down a street it will be my fault because I was alone.

My daughters are growing up in a society which demeans them as less than human. Their father has pornography in his home. I discovered it and was very shocked, and I was very afraid and I can't do anything about it except to be afraid and wait and watch.

And so for me listening to the stories that I heard earlier this evening, I felt very privileged because I haven't been raped by anybody since I was a kid, you know, I haven't been raped silently by a stranger. My daughters have not been raped and I hope they will not be. I have taken them to self-defense class.

Yet this is the kind of effect that pornography has on me: that I am constantly informed that it is okay to beat women and it is okay to rape women and women like being subjected to violence. And every time I step outside of my door and and every time I stay inside my house, I know that I may be the victim of violence against me, whether if be an obscene phone call or physical attack.

And all I have to say applies not only to that porn which depicts violent acts, I feel the same about pornography which merely shows women's genitals without the rest of their bodies. I have not seen anything depicting men's genitals with the rest of their bodies missing. Thank you.

MR. DAUGHTERY: Thank you.

Next we have William Prock, 818 Southeast Seventh Street.

William Prock: administrative burden of enforcement

MR. PROCK: That is correct. I am employed by the City of Minneapolis. I am the investigation manager for the Minneapolis Department of Civil Rights. I am not presenting a series of comments or position statements for the Department, I am aware that our Executive Director, George Caldwell, has certain questions and certain disagreements with me. I am aware that other people on our staff have other concerns, other questions, and we may or may not be in agreement.

What I would like to present is not to talk about sexual abuse, pornography per se. I would like to talk about the proposal before the Commission in the context of the Civil Rights statutes and in particular in relationship to the Minneapolis Civil Rights ordinance. Some of these concerns were heard yesterday and I anticipate a good session tomorrow afternoon, when I understand we are making a presentation to the Department.

The nation and the City of Minneapolis have a long history of concern for the rights of their citizens. These rights are embodied in the Constitution of the United States and the 50 states themselves. Unfortunately, we do not have the same history in ensuring that all citizens receive the opportunity to exercise those constitutionally guaranteed rights.

These constitutionally guaranteed rights are inherent in us as human citizens of the United States. As such, they are moral imperatives to all persons within the country. The concept of human rights and civil rights are not one and the same.

While human rights carry moral imperative, civil rights are those ensured by statute, statutes enacted in a limited fashion, to render real concepts embodied in the Constitution. Statutory civil rights, particularly those which resulted from the struggle exemplified by Dr. Martin Luther King, Junior, were enacted to provide a means of redress, for the denial of rights embodies in the statutes themselves. These rights all dealt with some aspect of life, the denial of which could produce some identifiable and concrete personal loss to the individual such as denial of a job, housing, the inability to obtain credit, inability to purchase a mean in a place of one's choice, inability to attend a movie theater, use a washroom, ride a bus, obtain an education and a myriad of other concrete harms.

Thus, Civil Rights statutes have in common the need to identify a specific identifiable and compensable harm to the individual in order to be able to invoke their protections. Further, each statute requires that a person claiming to be aggrieved be a member of a specifically identified protected class, race, sex, color, affectional preference et cetera. It is my opinion that the City of Minneapolis has one of the best drafted and comprehensive Civil Rights statutes in the country.

However, under the proposal before the Committee today, the concept of protected class is turned on its ear. We are no longer looking at a status

138

characteristic of an individual in order to obtain access to the laws' protection, rather we are dealing with an individual's behavior, the behavior of some other individual, or a graphic representation of behavior as the definitional basis for a new protected class.

While this may be legitimate, it is a new and untried legal approach and deserves, at minimum, the due deliberation given to all previous substantive amendments to the ordinance. I fight in particular the deliberation and time spent by the City Council on those amendments that added an affectional preference as a protected class in 1982 and permitted families with children to bring actions to the Civil Rights Department in the area of housing discrimination.

There are some specific concerns I have that result not in objections to the ordinance per se but as questions that I think the Council should consider in its deliberations. And I will do these by section. Section 2 (b)(1), this section provides that victims of pornography is another protected class, upon which a claim of employment, housing, and other forms of discrimination can be brought. And as such I believe —

MR. DAUGHTERY: Just a minute, what page are you on?

MR. PROCK: This is the first page, Section 2 (b)(1).

MR. DAUGHTERY: Go ahead.

MR. PROCK: This section, I believe, adds little or nothing in the way of further protection for women that already exists in the ordinance.

MS. MacKINNON: Mr. Prock, is sexual harassment a status characteristic?

MR. PROCK: No, it is not.

MS. MacKINNON: It is there.

MR. PROCK: It is a behavior that is directed — it is an obnoxious behavior. I understand that the pornography section is a theoretical extension of sexual harassment theory as interpreted through Title 7 and through the courts. Sexual harassment itself as under Section 7 is gender-free.

Okay, I don't want to debate because what I would like to do is raise the concerns and the Council will deal with them. Some of them, I believe, will have policy implications for the Council.

Section 3 (gg), pornography is so defined that a judgment of what is within that definition is either extremely broad and very easy, or extremely difficult, meaning that it is very narrow, with the potential for page by page and paragraph by paragraph analysis being required, and to the extreme requiring a percentage content rule to determine the inclusion or exclusion. This places a tremendous burden with the individuals charged with making those judgements. I believe in most cases the people making the judgements would be my staff in the Civil Rights Department. This is a burden that the City Council would not want to give to anyone without the proper legal counselling and background.

Section 4 (1), this defines what consists of trafficking in pornography. Prosecution under this section does not, as it is currently written and I interpret it, require any individual to come forward alleging concrete, identifiable and compensable harm under the law, as Civil Rights statutes

139

have been construed. The mere fact of production, regardless of the circumstances of that production, becomes a cause of action. The same would hold true for the sale, exhibition or distribution. No one need come forward and allege personal harm. This seems nothing more than an open attempt at ultimate censorship.

MS. HOYT: May I ask a question here?

MR. PROCK: Yes, ma'am.

MS. HOYT: What we are trying to say is that the existence of the material as described here is the harm.

MR. PROCK: I understand.

MS. HOYT: Do you understand that?

MR. PROCK: Yes, I understand that. I think the implication is that, as I read it, it is a risk. I am not saying tht this is gospel in any way, as I read it, the risk is that the mere sale, display et cetera would consitute a violation and would allow possibly the City Attorney's Office, my director, myself, any of my staff people essentially file the charge on sale, out it goes.

MS. HOYT: That is right.

MR. PROCK: I am not sure that will stand up.

MS. HOYT: Doesn't that make your job easier?

MR. PROCK: Unfortunately, it might make it much more difficult. I think it might make it much more difficult, I don't know. These are concerns I have.

I do believe, however, that the theory embodied in this particular section, and that is a body of literature and pictures or whatever, that deliberately and purposefully and with malice degrades and places into second-class citizenship a segment of our society and this is a rather dangerous theory. Under this theory it could be extended to the production, distribution, sale, or exhibition of literature produced by, in some cases, the Anti-Defamation League of the B'nai B'rith because it could in times degrade and put in second-class status non-Jewish citizens. Or it could be extended to permit the banning of publications for the National States Rights Party by directly and purposefully being aimed at perpetuating the second-class citizens of all racial minorities, particularly Black people. This is one of J. B. Stoner's [phonetic] publications. It could be interpreted to ban, should the theory hold, publications of the Black Panther Party if it ever comes back into the forefront, which are at times very degrading to whites.

In other instances it could in fact be extended to ban some of the publications of the American Civil Liberties Union, which in most cases do not reflect the opinions of the majority of Americans.

MS. HOYT: Could you tell me where in here that the material has to reflect the opinion of the majority of Americans?

MR. PROCK: I am not saying it is.

MS. HOYT: It was under my impression that the definition of pornography did not refer to the opinion of the majority of Americans.

MR. PROCK: That is correct. What I am trying to point out —

MS. HOYT: You seem to be going down a track that was not directed

140

at what was written in this ordinance. Are you saying this ordinance, you fear the passage of this ordinance would bring people to want to pass other —

MR. PROCK: I think that is a risk that is inherent in the theory that is embodied in the trafficking section.

While these last may seem far-fetched and impossible, the theory underlying the trafficking provision is the basis for such outlandish possibilities.

Within the governmental library exemption is a puzzling inconsistency, it is assumed that when pornography is sold over the counter, controlled or free, it is being pervaded and purchased for less than noble purposes. However, when it is lent by or used within a public library, it is for research purposes and the damage it commits upon its reader somehow seems to miraculously disappear.

If pornography is damaging and dangerous, it is so whether obtained from a magazine rack or public library.

MS. MacKINNON: If we eliminated that section, what would you then say?

MR. PROCK: I don't know, I would have to take a look at that in context with the rest of this.

Further, the open display of pornography is defined as sex discrimination when the library does the displaying, thus making the libraries subject to suits by citizens of the City of Minneapolis, alleging sex discrimination, not trafficking but invoking pain and suffering and punitive damages and other compensative awards for damages.

Section 5 (m)(1), this provides for a five-year statute of limitations in the bringing of a discrimination suit under this proposal. This is more closely allied to statutes of limitation for criminal actions. The remainder of the prohibited acts in the existing ordinance require action to be brought within six months. Is it proper to single out one form of discrimination, within a single statute, as being deserving a longer statute of limitations than all others? I merely offer this for Council's consideration, as all other forms of prohibited discrimination are considered equally bad under the law.

Finally I must say I have other reservations about this statute, particularly with Section 7 (o) which grants the Civil Rights Department investigative authority over acts of discrimination that are part and parcel of criminal activity. Currently, the existing ordinance under Section 141.90 prohibits the Department from issuing a complaint or hearing any matter when the alleged discrimination is part of or arises out of an incident or occurrence which in itself could give rise to a criminal prosecution for the violation of any State Statute other than the State Act against Discrimination.

As Alderman White and Daughtery and Howard are aware, the repeal of this provision occupied much time for the Council and the Civil Rights Commission for several years. Ultimately, it was deemed by the Council that the exemption should remain in the ordinance. My question is now, has the Council changed its mind and does it now desire the Civil Rights

Department to investigate discrimination that is entwined with criminal activity, or does the Council desire to retain the prohibition that was put in the ordinance at least 10 years ago and reaffirmed in 1982?

Ultimately, I fully support the effort for providing an administrative, at low or no cost, enforcement mechanism for women who have suffered harm at the hands of pimps, pornographers, rapists, and et cetera. Too often, I believe, women can't pursue legitimate claims that would result in punishment of a person who used them as sexual objects, solely because they are women, due to the prohibitive costs of such actions.

I only believe that the current proposal will not achieve that end, and if carried forward without due dilligence for legal precedents and inconsistency with legal theory, it stands the risk of taking the effort back beyond ground zero.

I simply ask the Council to study this matter with the same thoroughness it studied the original Minneapolis Civil Rights Ordinance and all the substantive amendments that have since been enacted.

MS. DWORKIN: May I ask one question? It is a real question.

CHAIRMAN WHITE: Let's not —

MS. DWORKIN: It is not a debating question.

CHAIRMAN WHITE: Quickly, so we can get as many to speak.

MS. DWORKIN: Mr. Prock, I certainly look forward to our conversation time, I want to tell you that.

I want to know what you describe as the concrete harms, the harms that the Civil Rights law is to address, and I would like you to say whether or not you consider the loss of your right to your own body as a concrete harm?

MR. PROCK: Conceptually, yes. Legally I don't know.

MS. DWORKIN: And your life?

MR PROCK: Yes, it is covered under the Civil Rights Statute.

CHAIRMAN WHITE: Those that are still remaining to speak, I'm going to have to cut you down to just quickly. If you have got something to submit, please submit it so that we can get out of here at 9:00 o'clock.

How many of you are still left here? Okay. You go, please.

Trina Porte: need for action

MS. PORTE: My name is Trina Porte, 861 19th Avenue Southeast, Minneapolis.

I have not yet been raped. At least, I have not been physically forced to have sex with men, which is not to say I have not been emotionally and psychologically coerced into having sex with men. I have. But that is not why I am speaking now.

I am speaking as someone who carefully listened to the testimony all yesterday afternoon and evening and I was astonished by all the people, who were mostly men, who said that they object to this ordinance because it might actually do something, because it might affect some examples of pornography as here very specifically defined.

They felt that we should be satisfied with laws as they now exist. Laws

142

written by and for men's use for the protection of their speech, actions and/or livelihood.

Yes, this ordinance might actually allow people to do something to address and maybe provide a means of redress for some of the unending violence done to women, children, and anyone else who has a case as defined very specifically in this ordinance.

That is why this ordinance needs to be passed, because it might just possibly do something to alleviate some of the violence that each and every woman must live with every day of her life just because she was born a woman.

CHAIRMAN WHITE: I want to thank all of you.

MS. HOYT: Chairman White?

CHAIRMAN WHITE: Alderman Hoyt?

Ms. Hoyt: incidence of crime near pornography sources

MS. HOYT: I would like to put one more thing in our records that I asked to be brought. As you know, we have in our Crime Prevention Department the ability to get sites, specific locations, and just one day I gave them the addresses of the bookstores that traffic in pornography and the movie houses in Minneapolis, some of them. And I asked them to run a site, specifically within one mile, since last June of the number of instances that we have had crimes that have occurred around those locations.

I also fed into it a location of a family movie theater which is 3800 42nd Avenue South, the Riverview Terrace. And we have found that 424 Hennepin and 624 Hennepin were so close that it was run as 500 Hennepin Avenue, and there were 566 crimes; 1111 Hennepin Avenue, there were 694; Franklin and 10th Avenue, within one mile, there were 894; 401 East Hennepin was 178; 2938 Lyndale Avenue South was 557; 409 West Broadway was 365; 345 East Lake Street was 810; 1500 East Lake was 656; 741 East Lake Street was 873. My momentary control, and we can run it on the other theaters, of 3800 42nd Avenue South was 69.

CHAIRMAN WHITE: These are criminal acts against persons or —

MS. HOYT: Against persons of assault, aggravated, simple assault, rape, indecent exposure, the sex crimes as they are put into our computers and I would like to enter this on the record. Thank you.

MS. DWORKIN: I have one final thing to put into evidence and it is a telegram from Gloria Steinem who says: "As someone who looks to Minnesota for national leadership in social policy, I urge you to amend Title 7 by including pornography as a form of sex discrimination. Your leadership is as historically important here as in making clear that rape is violence, not sexual expression or that sexual harassment is a major form of sexual discrimination." I will not read the rest of the telegram but I will enter this into evidence right now. Thank you.

CHAIRMAN WHITE: We are going to hear —

MS. MacKINNON: Ms. J says she wishes to testify.

CHAIRMAN WHITE: She wishes to testify, please make it brief.

MS. K: My name is -- [spelling out of name deleted]. First of all I want to thank those Council members who are staying here and listening to all of us. I appreciate the time you are putting in. I also want to say that I think it is more outrageous that more of the Council did not consider these hearings a high enough priority to be here.

Originally I chose not to speak at this hearing, but to submit written testimony instead. After last night's hearing, I've changed my mind for two reasons.

After some of the testimony, specifically that of the Civil Rights Commissioner's, I'm fearful that this ordinance will be postponed and then pushed aside. I don't want to be a part of the group that throws up their hands and says there's nothing that can be done or we're already doing all we can.

Something else occurred to me last night. I have been sexually abused in one form or another since I was 13. I am now 26, that's half of my life and that's too long for me.

This statement that was originally submitted as written testimony is addressed to the Government Operations Committee.

"I am writing to express my support for passage of the proposed amendment to the Civil Rights Ordinance recognizing pornography as sex discrimination against women. I do believe there is a strong connection between the use and existence of pornography and violence against women. This belief comes not from scientific studies, but from my personal experiences.

"As an adolescent, I was sexually molested in my own home by a family member who regularly used pornographic materials. I have been threatened at knifepoint by a stranger in an attempted rape. I have been physically and verbally harassed on the street, in other public places, and over the telephone at all hours of the night. I have experienced and continue to experience the humiliation, degradation and shame that these acts were meant to instill in me.

"I believe that the only difference between my experiences and pornography was the absence or presence of a camera. This connection became clear to me when I saw a documentary about pornography called *Not a Love Story*. I realized that I was any one of the women in the film, at least in the eyes of those men who have abused me. I saw myself through the abusers' eyes and I felt dirty and disgusting, like a piece of meat. It was the same shame and humiliation as in the other experiences. It didn't matter that it was only a movie.

"The message that pornography carries is clear to me. There is no place in our society where it is safe to be a woman, not in our homes, not in the streets, not even within our families. Pornography promotes and creates the conditions that make it dangerous to be a woman.

"I don't believe that it has to be this way. I hope this committee will strongly support these proposed amendments. Recognizing pornography as sex discrimination against women is the first step in some day making it safe to be a woman in our society." Thank you.

CHAIRMAN WHITE: I would like to thank all of you who also sat through and listened. It has been quite an experience. I have had quite a few experiences in my life that I will never forget, I have been here some time on this earth. This is one of those experiences that will live with me until I shuffle off. I want to thank you once again for coming out and we will do whatever we can possibly do, those of us that are here. This is part of the committee.

And for those of you who don't know, Councilmember Sally Howard had to leave and Councilmember Charlee Hoyt is here at my right and at my extreme right is Councilmember Daughtery, Pat Daughtery. Hopefully, together we can gather enough votes to get it through the Council. We are not going to promise you except one thing, and I think I am speaking for all of us, that we will do our very, very best to get this ordinance through this Council. Thank you all very much.

MS. HOYT: Mr. Chairman, may we move this ordinance for a special meeting on Thursday for discussion and Committee as to the action, tomorrow?

CHAIRMAN WHITE: You make that a motion.

MS. HOYT: I would like to move that.

CHAIRMAN WHITE: Thursday morning. Time?

MS. HOYT: 9:00, 9:30.

CHAIRMAN WHITE: 9:15.

MS. HOYT: So that the reason we will move it to a special meeting at 9:15 on Thursday so that there will be an opportunity for the Civil Rights Commission to have a chance to talk with and give us their suggestions. We would like to ask if our consultants can be present at our meeting on Thursday, and any other aldermen that wants to come.

MR. DAUGHTERY: I think we should ask the City Attorney also.

MS. MacKINNON: Allen Hyatt also.

CHAIRMAN WHITE: On the motion, the motion is to move —

MS. HOYT: To move the ordinance to a special meeting Thursday at 9:15.

CHAIRMAN WHITE: 9:15 All in favor say aye.

COMMITTEE MEMBERS: Aye.

CHAIRMAN WHITE: Opposed?

(No response.)

MS. MacKINNON: I would appreciate a statement from you on the record that everyone that signed up and who requested to speak at this hearing was allowed to speak. And that the hearings were brought to a close at a point at which no person indicated they further wished to speak.

CHAIRMAN WHITE: Let the record so show.

MS. MacKINNON: Thank you, Chairman.

MS. HOYT: I would also like to say I appreciate the fact that the consultants which the City Attorney's Office hired to construct and put together a public hearing which would give us the legal base we needed and allowed the input from all sectors of Minneapolis have done so. And I would like to publicly thank them and the City Attorney's Office and Al

145

Hyatt who has worked very hard to bring us this far. Thank you.
  (Hearing concluded.)